Fierce Feminine Divinities of Eurasia and Latin America

FIERCE FEMININE DIVINITIES OF EURASIA AND LATIN AMERICA

Baba Yaga, Kālī, Pombagira, and Santa Muerte

MałgorzataOles zkiewicz-Peralba

FIERCE FEMININE DIVINITIES OF EURASIA AND LATIN AMERICA
Copyright © Małgorzata Oleszkiewicz-Peralba, 2015.
Softcover reprint of the hardcover 1st edition 2015 978-1-137-54354-7

All rights reserved.

First published in 2015 by
PALGRAVE MACMILLAN®
in the United States—a division of St. Martin's Press LLC,
175 Fifth Avenue, New York, NY 10010.

Where this book is distributed in the UK, Europe and the rest of the world, this is by Palgrave Macmillan, a division of Macmillan Publishers Limited, registered in England, company number 785998, of Houndmills, Basingstoke, Hampshire RG21 6XS.

Palgrave Macmillan is the global academic imprint of the above companies and has companies and representatives throughout the world.

Palgrave® and Macmillan® are registered trademarks in the United States, the United Kingdom, Europe and other countries.

ISBN 978-1-349-56076-9   ISBN 978-1-137-53500-9 (eBook)
DOI 10.1057/9781137535009

Library of Congress Cataloging-in-Publication Data

Oleszkiewicz-Peralba, Malgorzata, 1954–
   Fierce feminine divinities of Eurasia and Latin America : Baba Yaga, Kali, Pombagira, and Santa Muerte / Malgorzata Oleszkiewicz-Peralba.
      pages cm
   Summary: "This provocative book examines untamed feminine divinities that are powerful, fiercely independent, courageous, and wise. They traverse time and national boundaries, appearing under different names all over the world. Although they have often been domesticated, maligned, and marginalized, they continue to be extremely attractive, as they empower their devotees confronting them with the ultimate reality of impermanence and death"—Provided by publisher.
   Includes bibliographical references and index.
       1. Goddesses. 2. Goddess religion. 3. Baba Yaga (Legendary character) 4. Kali (Hindu deity) 5. Pombagira (Afro-Brazilian deity) 6. Santa Muerte (Mexican deity) I. Title.

BL473.5.O54 2015
202'.114—dc23   2015009611

A catalogue record of the book is available from the British Library.

Design by Newgen Knowledge Works (P) Ltd., Chennai, India.

First edition: September 2015

10 9 8 7 6 5 4 3 2 1

*For all the women
who were dismissed and persecuted,
because of the gender,
their extraordinary abilities,
and their beliefs
For the Sisterhood*

Contents

List of Illustrations ix
Acknowledgments xiii

Introduction 1

Part I Eurasia

1 Baba Yaga, the Witch from Slavic Fairy Tales 15
2 Kālī, the Ultimate Fierce Feminine 53

Part II Latin America

3 Pombagira, the Holy Streetwalker 69
4 Santa Muerte, Death the Protector 103
Conclusion 137

Notes 143
Bibliography 159
Index 175

Illustrations

Figures

I.1	Goddess Coatlicue, Mexico City	2
1.1	Baba Yaga by Maya Sokovic	16
1.2	*Tapísde la creació* (Tapestry of creation), Girona Cathedral, Spain	24
1.3	The Mesoamerican feathered serpent, Quetzalcoatl, Mexico City	29
1.4	ContemporaryB ulgarianM artenitsas	32
1.5	PolishM arzanna	45
1.6	Goddess motifs on shirt embroideries, Poland, beginning of the twentieth century	47
1.7	The goddess as the Lady of the Heavens, the Earth, and the Underworld, paper cutout, Poland	47
1.8	The goddess as the tree of life, paper cutout, Poland	48
1.9	The goddess accompanied by growing plants, flowers, and celestial bodies, paper cutout, Łowicz region, Poland, beginning of the twentieth century	48
1.10	Two birds on a tree, paper cutout, Poland	49
1.11	Thegodde ss Żywa accompanied by growing plants, paper cutout, Łowicz region, Poland, end of the nineteenth century	50
2.1	Kālī by Maya Sokovic	60
2.2	Processionf orS ara-La-Kâli,Le sS aintes Maries-de-la-Mer, France, 2008	65

3.1	Pombagira house altar, Salvador, Bahia, Brazil,1996	71
3.2	Altar with Sara Kali, Jesus Christ, and Nossa Senhora Aparecida, Tzara Ramirez, Rio de Janeiro, Brazil, 2009	78
3.3	Gypsy entities incarnated into mediums practice "charity," Tzara Ramirez, Rio de Janeiro, Brazil, 2009	79
3.4	Barô Marcelo in front of his Candomblé *terreiro*, Rio de Janeiro, Brazil, 2009	80
3.5	Exu Zé Pilintra at Marcelo's *terreiro*, Rio de Janeiro, Brazil, 2009	81
3.6	Pombagira Cigana at Marcelo's *terreiro*, Rio de Janeiro, Brazil, 2009	82
3.7	Symbols of Exu at Marcelo's *terreiro*, Rio de Janeiro, Brazil, 2009	82
3.8	Dulcified image of goddess Iemanjá, Salvador, Bahia, Brazil, 1996	84
3.9	Representation of Exu, Rio de Janeiro, Brazil, 2009	86
3.10	Umbanda offering at the beach, Angra dos Reis, Brazil,2009	90
3.11	*Povo da rua*: Pombagira and Exu, Rio de Janeiro, Brazil,2009	91
4.1	Santa Muerte wearing a Franciscan monk's cape, Piedras Negras, Mexico, 2008	104
4.2	Santa Muerte seated on a throne, San Antonio, United States, 2012	105
4.3	Santa Muerte wearing a bride's gown, Mercado de Sonora, Mexico City, 2009	106
4.4	"Aztec" Santa Muerte, San Antonio, United States, 2012	107
4.5	Seven-colored Santa Muerte, San Antonio, United States, 2012	108
4.6	SantaM uerte *veladora*, San Antonio, United States, 2012	109

4.7	Santa Muerte products, Botánica Papa Jim's, San Antonio, United States, 2012	109
4.8	Santa Muerte covered in dollar bills, Mercado de Sonora, Mexico, 2009	110
4.9	Santa Muerte as the Virgin of Guadalupe, cover, *La biblia de la Santa Muerte*(n.d.)	111
4.10	Santa Muerte and Guadalupe, Botánica Papa Jim's, San Antonio, United States, 2012	116
4.11	SantaM uertea ndGua dalupe,bot ánica, San Cristóbal de las Casas, Mexico, 2014	117
4.12	Cihuateteo,M exicoC ity	128
4.13	Altar for the Dead, San Antonio, United States,20 12	129
4.14	Lowrider, Lowrider Festival, San Antonio, United States, 2012	130
4.15	Lowrider trunk altar for the dead with Santa Muerte, Centro Cultural Aztlán, San Antonio, United States, 2012	131

TABLE

3.1	Continuum of Afro-Brazilian religions	93

Acknowledgments

I wish to express my deep gratitude to the people and institutions who supported me as this book took shape throughout the years. To Sam Pochucha for his continuous assistance and review of the many versions of my manuscript, and to Dr. Alan West-Durán for his conscientious reading of the manuscript and his valuable comments.

Special thanks to my informants from Tzara Ramirez and Templo dos Ciganos Encantados in Rio de Janeiro, as well as from Ilê Asé Orisanlá J'Omin Terreiro in Salvador, Bahia, for their generosity, trust, and enthusiasm in sharing their practices with me, as well as to all the people in Brazil who helped me in the performance of my research and offered support in my endeavors.

I am grateful to the staff from the State Ethnographic Museum in Warsaw and the Łowicz Museum, Poland, for their assistance and liberality in granting me access to their collections. To my late father, Eligiusz Oleszkiewicz, for his support in finding and translating Russian sources, and to my family in Poland for their interest in my project and for their practical help. To my San Antonio and Mexico City informants, as well as to all the persons who facilitated my research travels to Mexico, for their generosity.

I am indebted to the University of Texas at San Antonio, particularly the College of Liberal and Fine Arts Dean's office, and the Department of Modern Languages and Literatures for making my research possible through faculty development leaves, course releases, and awards to conduct fieldwork in different locations. To my graduate research assistants for finding and scanning many of the sources and for compiling the initial bibliography, and to the Department of Art and Art History for their technical help.

I owe thanks to my editors at Palgrave Macmillan, Robyn Curtis, Shaun Vigil, and Erica Buchman for their professional guidance throughout the review and publication process, to Deepa John at Newgen Knowledge Works for her masterful editorship, and to my anonymous reviewers for their thoughtful suggestions. To Dr. Eva Bueno for counsel in my Portuguese queries, and to Maya Sokovic for drawing original images for my book. To my friends in the San Antonio area and the West Coast for their interest, enthusiasm, and inspiration, and to Dr. Josep Maria Peralba for his continuous support, encouragement, and trust in me and in the importance of this project.

* * *

ALL TRANSLATIONS, unless otherwise indicated, are mine.

Introduction

O Devī, you who remove the sufferings of your suppliants, be gracious. Be propitious, O Mother of the whole world. Be gracious, O Mother of the universe. You are, O Devī, the ruler of all that is moving and unmoving. You are the sole substratum of the world.

—Devī-māhātmyam, Ch. 11: 3 and 4

*I've heard the hue of Her skin is a dark
That lights the world.*

—Sen6 1

For years, I have been studying divine feminine figures from different cultures, and in 2007 and 2009, I published the book *The Black Madonna in Latin America and Europe: Tradition and Transformation*. In addition to well-known, benign female divinities discussed in this book, such as the Christian Virgin Mary and the Brazilian Candomblé Oxum, as well as the Hindu Lakṣmī, during my fieldwork I discovered a whole gamut of their contrasting, but not so widely known, marginal, fierce counterparts, such as the Russian/Polish Baba Yaga, the Indian Kālī, the Brazilian Pombagira, and the Mexican Santa Muerte. Although distant geographically, they are surprisingly similar. All of them represent the concepts of liminality, outsiderhood, and structural inferiority,[1] embodied in the divine feminine. These goddesses are strong, independent, unrestrained, and full of extraordinary, magical powers, including power over sexuality, transformation, and death. In fact, they are the opposite of what has been promoted as the model for Western females in the past millennium, with traits such as motherliness, docility, humility, passivity, and obedience. In *Fierce Feminine Divinities of Eurasia and Latin America*, I examine these untamed, outsider counterpart divinities that, in contrast, are powerful, fiercely independent, childless, courageous, and wise. They traverse time and national boundaries, appearing under different names all over the world, from Europe to Asia, and the Americas. Even their iconography is surprisingly similar. For example, Baba Yaga, Kālī, Santa Muerte, as well as Coatlicue (figure I.1)[2]—deities from three different continents—are all portrayed adorned with human skulls, bones, and often snakes.

Figure I.1 Goddess Coatlicue, Mexico City. Photo by author

Each of these four figures can be defined as liminal, marginal, as well as alternative, and correspondences may be traced between them and the liminal/marginal status of their worshippers. The concept of liminality as "transition" was first introduced by the Belgian folklorist Arnold van Gennep in his 1908 book titled *Les rites de passage*. He described the recurring pattern of the rites of passage or transition rites as those that accompany a change of social status, age, or location, among others, and that include a process of separation, transition, and incorporation. This concept, introduced to the Anglo-Saxon audience with the 1960 translation of his book, was rediscovered and further developed as "liminality" by Victor Turner in his books *The Forest of Symbols* (1967), *The Ritual Process* (1969), and *Dramas, Fields, and Metaphors* (1974). Currently, liminality is considered a key concept in social and political sciences and has been further elaborated by Arpad Szakolczai and Bjorn Thomassen, among others. It encompasses both space and time. As Thomassen asserts:

> Single moments, longer periods, or even whole epochs can be liminal. Liminal spaces can be specific thresholds; they can also be more extended areas, like "borderlands" or, arguably, whole countries, placed in important in-between positions between larger civilizations. Liminality can also be applied to both single individuals and to larger groups...or whole societies, or maybe evenc ivilizations.(16)

Based on his studies of the Ndembu culture of northwestern Zambia, Turner made a distinction between the three stages of a rite of passage, namely, separation (old status), liminality (no clear-cut status), and reincorporation (new status). This process is most clearly observable during ritual initiation, but can be applied to any change of status, such as marriage, graduation, death, or a territorial passage. The term "liminality" itself comes from the Latin *limen* ("threshold") and *limes* ("limit") and indicates a state in between structure, which is characterized by ambiguity and ambivalence and is usually connected to marginality, inferiority, as well as to ritual powers. These are also conditions in which myths, symbols, and rituals may be generated (Turner, *Ritual* 128–30).

In his *Dramas, Fields, and Metaphors*, Turner further emphasizes three aspects of culture specially "endowed with ritual symbols and beliefs of non-social-structural type": "liminality," "outsiderhood," and "structural inferiority." A related term is "marginality," as marginals are similar to liminars in that they are in the ambiguous state of "betwixt and between"; nevertheless, they have little perspective of any resolution of that state. For Turner, marginals include individuals who are members of two or more social groups whose cultural norms are contrasting with one another, migrant workers from country to country or from country to city, second-generation immigrants, women in nontraditional roles, parvenus, and déclassés. In a word, their situation excludes them from any accepted or clearly defined social group. While "*liminality* [as originally described] represents the midpoint of transition in a status-sequence between two positions, *outsiderhood* refers to actions and relationships which do not flow from a recognized social status but originate outside it." This includes persons such as shamans, mediums, monks, hippies, and gypsies. "Lowermost status" or "structural inferiority," on the other hand, "refers to the lowest rung in a system of social stratification in which unequal rewards are accorded" (231–37).

The aforementioned notions especially apply to the twentieth and the twenty-first centuries in which large populations have been displaced and forced to migrate, or even to adopt a nomadic lifestyle, because of economic, political, social, and legal unsettlement. These individuals may spend their entire lives in a marginalized and transient state, devoid of economic, political, and social rights, as are the impoverished inhabitants of Brazilian *favelas*, many Mexican *colonias*, and particularly the "illegal aliens" on the Mexico-US borderlands. These individuals construct alternative economies as well as symbols and spaces of worship outside the official channels of church and state.

The four divine figures I discuss in this book may be seen as embodiments of liminality and marginality with many of their attributes, such as being outsiders and being connected to liminal activities (e.g., messenger, trickster, sexuality). They are also perceived as dangerous, uncomfortable, rejected, or representing the rejected, but at the same time attractive, as they embody wisdom, magical powers, and the truth of human condition. They appear in regions of the world that are considered marginal—Eastern Europe, South-Central Asia, and Latin America—in that they are located far from the world power centers. Moreover, the deities themselves inhabit places at the margins of "civilization" within these regions, such as forests, crossroads, and cemeteries, and their worshippers generally reside in poor, peripheral neighborhoods and are frequently considered outsiders.

Their liminality as well as the one of their worshippers may be spatial, temporal, or both. By Turner's expression, these deities may be described as being in a "limbo of statuslessness." In fact, they embody the paradox of a permanent liminal status.[3] Such liminal personae or "threshold people" elude any classifications, as they have no official status, their attributes are indeterminate, and they may be expressed by symbols, such as death, being in the womb, invisibility, darkness, bisexuality, and wilderness, as well as sacredness (Turner, *Ritual* 95–97).

The unrestrained, threshold divinities I analyze in this book have been present in the history of humanity for at least as long as the ones that are currently accepted or culturally sanctioned, but they have been marginalized, demonized, sweetened, domesticated, or relegated to fairy tales, children's games, and jokes. Today, they are reemerging in old and new forms. Some of them, like the Hindu Kālī, have been widely known under their current names but expanded geographically with the Indian diaspora to England and the West Indies; and others, such as the Brazilian Pombagira, are New World syncretic creations that absorbed local entities as well as those from Africa and Europe, after their Atlantic migrations.

All these fierce, outsider deities are connected to the witch archetype; initially, the witch was a wise, holy woman, a matriarch, folk doctor, and seer. In fact, the English word "pharmacy" derives from the Greek *pharmakeia* ("use of drugs," "witchcraft") and *pharmakis* (fem.)/*pharmakeus* (masc.) ("preparer of drugs," "witch," "sorcerer") ("Pharmacy"). The transformation of the wise goddess into a malevolent hag or crone is reflected in the etymology of the word "witch" in different Indo-European languages. For example, the English "witch" comes from the Anglo-Saxon *wicca/wicce*, a corruption of *witega* ("seer" "diviner"), and the Icelandic *vitki* ("witch") comes from *vita* ("to know").[4] Similarly, the Russian *ved'ma* and the Polish *wiedźma* ("witch") originally meant "the one who knows," from the verbs *vedat'* (Russ.) and *wiedzieć* (Pol.) ("to know").[5] The connection of these figures to knowledge and wisdom is widely documented in many cultures. They have also been believed to possess supernatural powers of transformation, to be able to change themselves and others into different beings and forms. Nevertheless, today these traditional wise women are called "hags," "crones," and "witches"—words carrying a heavy, negative, and demeaning load. They are synonymous with old, ugly, withered, and ill-tempered women, especially repulsive within modern Western culture that overvalues youth and perfection in external appearance.[6] Thus, the wise goddess, once a central, all-encompassing persona, became its antithesis—the lowest and most disdained member of society—and has frequently been demonized. There are still countries such as India, where connections with death, sexuality, and rage are generally not considered "negative," but a necessary part of the life cycle. This can be seen in the veneration of the goddess Kālī, but even there, she is frequently dulcified.[7] In Slavic regions, where Baba Yaga likely used to be a form of the primordial bird-snake goddess, she has been relegated to the witch role in children's fairy tales. On the other hand, in countries like Brazil and Mexico, where large segments of the population live outside the official economy and culture, or are subjected to extreme dangers, entities like Pombagira and Santa Muerte, respectively, which embody these otherwise unpopular qualities, have gained wide following, mainly among subaltern classes and among certain occupations.

In *Fierce Feminine Divinities of Eurasia and Latin America*, I apply the aforementioned concepts and symbols and seek to understand why these divinities have been so transformed. I discuss and demonstrate the similarities and differences and the symbolic significance and implications of the earlier mentioned figures for women and world cultures, in order to increase the understanding of different perspectives and traditions by which women have been regarded. In addition, I analyze the social processes that accompany cultural and religious change in Europe, Asia, and Latin America.

Chapter 1, "Baba Yaga, the Witch from Slavic Fairy Tales," examines the figure of Baba Yaga, possibly a pre-Slavic goddess of death and regeneration who, with time and changing socio-economic conditions, was converted into a malevolent witch that today only appears in fairy tales and folklore. Nevertheless, studies have shown that these magical tales (Russian *volshebnye skazki*) are a remnant of ancient religious ritual practices in which Baba Yaga played an important role as a facilitator in life passages, such as initiation into adulthood and death. She is a liminal deity par excellence, dwelling between the world of the living and of the dead, who has female, male, and animal characteristics, abilities of transformation, and is dual—both terrifying and beneficial. Moreover, her hut that stands on birds' feet in a dense forest is constructed from human body parts. I analyze the symbolism of these mysterious elements surrounding Baba Yaga in order to unravel her original function, while making references to other demonized goddesses from different cultures.

Chapter 2, "Kālī, the Ultimate Fierce Feminine," discusses manifestations of Mother Goddess cosmic energy, *śakti*, focusing on the goddess Kālī's worship in India and its ramifications in the West Indies. In addition, the connections between this Hindu goddess and the prehistoric Baba Yaga, the Indian Dhūmāvatī, as well as the Brazilian holy harlot, Pombagira, and the Mexican Santa Muerte are discussed. Her link to Pombagira is particularly strong as it has been reported that in northern areas of India, such as Kangra and Bengal, the goddess (Vaishno Deva, Jrala Mukhi, Durgā, and Kālī) with her divine energy *śakti*, enters women in possession trances during which the mediums speak.[8] Such possession rituals play an important role in women's empowerment in the case of Kālī as well as of Pombagira.

Chapter 3 focuses on the entity "Pombagira, the Holy Streetwalker" from the twentieth-century Brazilian Umbanda religion. This figure has its origins in the European wise women and the pan-African Ìyàmi Òṣòròngà, both degraded as "witches," as well as in the god Bombonjira, a Congo name for the Yoruba trickster and mediator god Exu. In contemporary Brazil, Pombagira is the female counterpart of Exu and is portrayed as a street woman with all her vices and strength—an epitome of "the other." She appears when Umbanda initiates enter into trances embodying her. Similarly to Baba Yaga, this powerful entity has been identified with a female devil, but simultaneously invoked for strength, protection, and support. She is a representation of a prostitute, an independent woman who has "seven husbands" and does not accept male domination. As is Kālī, Pombagira is associated with transition and dangerous places, such as the crossroads, the cemetery, and garbage deposits, as well as with possession trances, advice giving, blood sacrifice, alcohol, and the colors red and black.

Chapter 4, "Santa Muerte, Death the Protector," examines this Latin American unofficial saint who, similar to Pombagira, is related to liminality, scarcity, and conflict. Worship of Santa Muerte started to be widespread in Mexico City about 20 years ago, especially in the marginal neighborhood of Tepito in the *colonia* Morelos, but later extended to surrounding areas and countries, from Central America in the south to the United

States in the north. Although the veneration of death has ancient Native Mexican roots in the gods of the underworld, Mictlantecuhtli and Mictlancíhuatl, the Santa Muerte persona is mainly based upon medieval European fascination with death and her all-embracing Latin American colonial imagery. Nevertheless, this cult[9] changed in character, and today it is popular especially among liminal sectors of population that deal with transitions and transgressions, such as people working on the streets (e.g., street vendors, criminals, and prostitutes), migrants, inmates, policemen, troops, prison guards, social workers, and lawyers. Moreover, the worship of Santa Muerte is connected to transnational drug trafficking.

Santa Muerte, like Baba Yaga, Kālī, and Pombagira, is an untamed feminine deity. All four of them are strongly connected to marginality, ambiguity, sacred powers, transformation and transmutation of matter, the passage from life to death, and vice versa. They are either accompanied by symbols of death, such as skulls, bones, entrails, and blood, or they are portrayed as a skeleton, as in the case of Santa Muerte. Baba Yaga is a demonized ancient deity that helps in this passage, standing in the threshold between life and death; Kālī is a fierce warrior who performs a winning battle with demons and is often portrayed as emaciated; Pombagira is the lady of cemeteries; and Santa Muerte is death itself. Their favorite dwelling places are a hut in a deep forest and a bridge over a river of fire—symbols of liminality and the passage to the other world—in the case of Baba Yaga; places of battle and cremation grounds in the case of Kālī; crossroads and cemeteries in the case of Pombagira; and all marginal, transition places for Santa Muerte. The liminality of these figures is both spatial and temporal, as they are often linked to the outskirts and to the transition between day and night; this reflects the social marginalization of large groups of their devotees, especially in Latin America. These icons are also connected to blood and regeneration, sometimes requiring blood sacrifice. In addition, both Pombagira and Kālī are linked to possession trances, usually performed by women. In the tales, Baba Yaga cooks and consumes human flesh, thus transforming matter, but she is also in the business of reuniting young couples for procreation. Kālī eats human flesh and drinks blood, and by dwelling at cremation grounds she also transmutes matter; Pombagira is connected to human sexuality as well as to blood and death, thus containing the life cycle; and Santa Muerte embodies death itself, but she is also invoked for good luck and miracles in love, as her initial function in the mid-twentieth century, when she emerged on the streets of Mexico City, is said to have been love magic, similar to the case of Pombagira.

My book on feminine divinities across cultures and continents that encompasses and compares the Slavic Baba Yaga, the Hindu goddess Kālī, the Brazilian Pombagira, and the Mexican Santa Muerte responds to and reflects a growing interest in liminal, fierce feminine archetypes and syncretic religions. Not only are these figures similar in their powers and external attributes, but there are strong analogies in the types and locations of people who worship them, in the ways they do, and in the spiritual, psychological, and sociological implications of this veneration. My study observes and calls attention to these similarities that have been overlooked in the past, addressing fundamental questions of culture, such as people's migrations, transculturation, and adaptation, and examines how their sacred icons adjusted and transformed. It bridges places and times as it links three continents as well as prehistoric times with contemporaryphe nomena.[10]

Fierce Feminine Divinities of Eurasia and Latin America is based on my fieldwork in Afro-Brazilian religious communities (Rio de Janeiro and Salvador, Brazil, in 2009 and in 1996), in Mexican and Mexican American devotions to Santa Muerte (Mexico City, Piedras Negras, San Cristóbal de las Casas, and San Antonio from 2008 to 2014), and in Slavic and Baltic popular religiosity and folklore (Poland, Russia, and Lithuania throughout the 1990s, the 2000s, and the 2010s), as well as on extensive archival and library research on these topics and on the goddess Kālī. It is intended for scholars and students in the areas of women's studies, comparative religions, mythology, Latin American studies, Afro-Latin American studies, Slavic studies, transnational cultural studies, anthropology, as well as for the general public.

PART I

Eurasia

CHAPTER 1

Baba Yaga, the Witch from Slavic Fairy Tales

In the Slavic lands of Europe and Eurasia, there is an ancient deity that shares various traits with the Indian goddess Kālī, the Brazilian Pombagira, and the Mexican Santa Muerte. Her name is Baba Yaga (Yegi Baba, Baba Jaga, Jaga Yagishna, Baba Jędza, Babaroga, etc.); and although various scholars have demonstrated that she and her tales are remnants of ancient religious and ritual practices,[1] currently she is only found in fairy tales and folklore, portrayed as a repulsive hag that frightens children (figure 1.1).

In this chapter, I analyze the symbolism of the mysterious elements surrounding the figure of Baba Yaga in order to unravel her origins, her connection to other holy personae, and the reasons for her demonization. As she is currently not an object of devotion anywhere, this chapter is based on my analysis of Slavic fairy tales, mainly compiled by Aleksandr Afanas'ev in the nineteenth century, and on critical texts.

Liminality

Similarly to the Zambian Ndembu novices undergoing initiation, described by Victor Turner, the holy figures analyzed in this book dwell in a state of liminality. Inhabiting a sacred spacetime, they are liberated from structural obligations and are connected to the powers of life and death ("Liminal to Liminoid" 59). A particularly strong example of a liminal persona is the

Figure 1.1 Baba Yaga by Maya Sokovic. Reproduced with permission of the artist

paradoxical Baba Yaga who exists in a permanent state of in-betweenness, encompassing many opposites. She dwells between life and death, youth and old age, human and animal, male and female, as well as "good" and "bad" characteristics. Her symbols are drawn from the biology of death and decomposition, she can be considered sexless or bisexual, her features are exaggerated, her hut is both tomb- and womb-like, and both her appearance and her actions are the embodiment of ambiguity and paradox. In addition, she is accompanied by fragments, such as body parts that are recombined into unusual compositions, for example, a fence of human skulls or a door lock made of a jaw with sharp teeth. This reduction to substance symbolizes her all-encompassing, universal nature (Turner, *Forest* 95–110), and these characteristics, exemplified in the fairy tales, point to the original sacredness of Baba Yaga.

Death, Fragmentation, and Transformation

Today, Baba Yaga is the main character of Slavic magical or fairy tales and is identified with an ugly and malevolent witch or *ved'ma* (Russ.)/*wiedźma* (Pol.). Nevertheless, as Vladimir Propp demonstrated, she also plays the main donor or benevolent role in these tales.[2] In fact, Baba Yaga may be portrayed as (1) a good and wise, foretelling old woman who helps the hero; (2) a bad woman who abducts children, persecutes the hero, and threatens him with death; and sometimes (3) a fighter (Toporov 30). This apparent dual or even triune portrayal of Baba Yaga is due to the fact that this character encompasses more than just one sphere. She is connected to the heavens, the earth, and the underworld, as well as to the past, the present, and the future, to life and to death. Her association with the heavens is symbolized by her bird features, and with the underworld by the serpent and the oven. Russian scholars, such as Propp and Toporov, were convinced that the origin of the fairy tale is to be found in ancient religion and ritual. Many of the characters of the magical tales were first religious figures, and the actions performed by them were connected to primordial rituals, such as initiation, body inhumation, and burning. As it can be deduced from her similarity to the Black Goddess of death and regeneration, as well as from many other traits contained in the fairy tales, discussed further in this chapter, originally Baba Yaga was a mighty earth goddess with dominion over life, death, regeneration, time, and the elements, similar to the Indian Kālī—the creator, preserver, and destroyer—and to the pan-African ancestral Mysterious Mother, Ìyàmi Òṣòròngà. Her appearance was often accompanied by strong winds, and her dwelling places were dark, mysterious birch forests. Baba

Yaga is connected to both death and growth. In the tales, she also appears as guardian of the Waters of Life and of Death. These waters help beings to become alive and grow or to die.[3] She lives in the dense forest in a hut placed on hens' feet or, in some tales, on a spindle that spins in conjunction with the phases of the moon.[4] Fragmentation is exemplified by her house, constructed from human body parts, surrounded with a fence made of bones topped with skulls that irradiate light at night, and an entrance guarded by a mouth with sharp teeth for a lock. In the tale "Vasilisa the Fair":

> Vasilisa walked all night and all day and long. Late on the second evening she arrived in the clearing where Baba Yaga's hut was standing. The fence around it was made of human bones. Skulls with empty eye sockets stared down from the posts. The gate was made from bones of human legs; the bolts were made from human hands; and the lock was a jaw with sharp teeth. (Tatar176)

Baba Yaga is also strongly linked to death and bone remains through her "bony leg" and her alter ego, the sorcerer Koshchey Bessmertnyi, whose name approximates "Bony the Deathless." In his extensive work *Prahistoria religii na ziemiach polskich* (Pre-History of Religion on Polish Lands), Włodzimierz Szafrański affirms that the most common mortuary practice in Neolitic Central Europe consisted in burials on wooden platforms placed on poles that were accompanied by inhumation, in order to dry and better preserve bone remains that where meticulously cared for. Later, this practice transformed into cremation, and the ashes were buried in the ground.[5] Toporov also posits that Baba Yaga's hut is closely related to *É ḫešta*, a Hittite "house of bones, bone remains," connected to the deity of the underworld kingdom of the dead, Lelwani.[6] Moreover, *É.NA* "stone house," where bone remains were protected and precious metals, as well as food for the dead, were stored, is almost identical to Baba Yaga's hut. In the hut from the *skazka* ("tale"), the hero is fed and Baba Yaga stores gold, silver, and copper—the treasures of the earth goddess, further discussed in chapter 3. In addition, her house stands up high, like Hittite receptacles with ash and bones of the dead, which were placed on poles (Toporov 35–37).

Baba Yaga, who travels in a mortar pushing herself with a pestle, removes her trace with a birch broom, as described in the tale "Vasilisa the Fair": "[T]here was Baba Yaga flying up in a mortar, swinging her pestle like a whip and sweeping the tracks away with a broom" (Alexander 145). The hut, as the earth, represents the universal egg, the womb of all creation (Hubbs 38–39), as well as the tomb. Interestingly, *pisanki* or boiled, painted eggs, which to this day are part of the Slavic Easter ritual, used to be the symbolic food of the dead. In Slavic tradition, it is believed that Mother Earth eats her own children. According to a Polish legend, "God ordered the Earth: 'You will give birth to people and you will devour them; whatever you give birth to, you will eat, as it is yours'" (Szyjewski 211, 130). Similar to the earth, Baba Yaga is a cannibal mother. In many tales, she lures children to her dwelling, in order to roast and eat them. These actions echo the practice of ritual cannibalism and resurrection magic found in Central Europe during the Paleolithic and the Mesolithic eras (Szafrański 54). She is a liminal, multiple, paradoxical, magical being, capable of transformation—she can appear as the old, wise woman, the lovely young maiden, and the doll, as in "Vasilisa the Fair."[7] It is interesting to note that the Hindu/Buddhist crone goddess Dhūmāvatī, discussed in chapter 2, has similar characteristics. This interchangeability is linked to Baba Yaga's function as goddess of life, death, and regeneration, represented by the trinity of goddesses—the maiden, the mother, and the crone— that changed into each other together with the cycles of life and nature. This process is reflected by traditional Slavic round dances named *korowody*.[8] The number "three" had a special significance for many cultures from the most remote of times. It is the most holy, perfect, and magical number of synthesis, which symbolizes the deity. It appears in many realms of life and is preserved in folklore, tales, and incantations (Kopaliński 433–35). Its pervading presence is exemplified by holy and human trinities: the three spheres of heaven, earth, and the underworld; the three times of dawn, midday, and night; as well as the three essential colors—white, red, and black—discussed further in this book.

As the mistress of all nature, the goddess of the tales and the embroideries is usually represented with and helped by animals. For example, in the tale "Go There I Know Not Where, Fetch That I Know Not What," Tsarevna Maria ("Princess Maria"), who is also Baba Yaga's daughter, has all the birds, beasts, fish, and other living things at her command (Alexander 180–203), and in the tale "Finist, the Bright Falcon," Mariushka is helped and protected by wolves, bears, foxes, and other wild animals (*Baśnie* 41). As discussed further in this chapter, creatures that dwell in several realms, such as birds and snakes, which deal with the skies, the earth, and the underworld, are especially important as mediators. The dragon or winged serpent (*zmei*—Russ., *żmij*—Pol.) is the most potent and feared of all, as it encompasses the three realms. Baba Yaga is also a mistress of horses and has a fire-breathing flying horse. Particularly, in the series of tales portraying the Baba Yaga–fighter type, she is accompanied by a horse, and sometimes she leads an army of Amazons, as in the battles of the legendary Tar Tarchovich, around 1,000 BC (Kohli 187). Not only do the three spheres of nature belong to her, but also all of its elements; like Ìyàmi Òṣòròngà described in chapter 3, she is the mistress of air, water, fire, and earth.

Because of their ritualistic origin, the tales that have suffered the least of transformations have to be understood at a symbolic level, as there is no explanation for the characters' actions in daily life. In fact, both at the beginning and at the end of the tales, there usually is a formula that sets them aside from daily life and lineal time, beyond the known world. A telling example is the beginning of the tale "The Firebird and Vasilisa-Tsarevna": "Once upon a time, beyond the thrice-nine land, in the thrice-tenth stardom."[9] This formula, as well as others included in the texts, such as "After a long or a short time the marksman came to the end of the world" separate the magical realm of the tales from ordinary reality, which is measured by precise time and space.[10] At the end of the tales, there is usually a humorous formula added, such as: "I too was at this feast and drank mead and wine which flowed down my beard, missing my mouth,"[11] which further reinforces the magical reality notion and perhaps was used to trivialize and camouflage the tales' content. Originally, stories and their dramatic representations were part of the initiation ritual itself. These esoteric origin-myths and their telling played magical functions and were subject to prohibitions. The spreading of these myths would have stripped them from their sacred character. At the time when the myths started to reappear in the tales, the themes and their narration were already separate from the actual rituals. The sacred became profane and the esoteric and religious were converted into artistic, literary creations. According to Propp, the ritual was alive when hunting was still the primary way of sustenance. The tale inherited these religious aspects, but the religion itself also underwent modifications with changing economic conditions (*Raíces* 526–35). According to Szafrański, during the upper Paleolithic and the Mesolithic period, hunter-gatherers were constituted into totemic clans that worshipped a mythic ancestor in the form of a bird or a wild horse. During a sacred banquet, they consumed the totem. This action, during which the deity was incorporated into the bodies of its worshippers, is symbolically equivalent to the consumption of the "body" and "blood" of Christ during the Holy Communion (49). As late as in the Middle Ages, in Russia and in other Slavic areas, the telling of certain magical tales was still part of a ritual performed only during a certain part of the year and day. The sacred nature of these gatherings is confirmed by the fact that they were condemned by church officials, for example, the twelfth-century priest St. Kirill of Turov.[12] Similar prohibitions in regard to collective telling of tales while spinning and weaving existed in other areas of Europe, such as Germany, as late as the sixteenth and seventeenth centuries (Kohli 21).

Baba Yaga's Name and Ritual Blindness

The name Baba Yaga (or Yaga Baba) is unique to Slavic cultures and languages[13] and can be traced to ancient times. The origin of the word "baba" is found in the Proto-Indo-European root b(h)ab(h). Today, its derivatives are still used in different Indo-European languages, such as the English "baby," the German *bube* ("boy"), the Italian *babbo* ("father"), the Lithuanian *boba* ("old woman") (Shapiro 112), and the Portuguese *babá* ("babysitter"). In Slavic languages, the shared meaning of "baba" is "grandmother," which derived into an "old, married, or peasant woman" and with time became derogatory, as an "old, ugly, fat woman." In Old Russian, "baba" was a midwife, sorceress, and future-teller (Johns 9). In Polish, there are other derivatives as well, such as *babka* ("little *baba*") or a "feisty female." The use of this word is widespread in Polish and has various meanings, from a special holiday pastry with a distinctly round, full shape and a hole in the middle to *babka piaskowa* with a similar shape, made by children from sand. The game "blind man's buff" is called *ślepa babka* ("blind *babka*") in Polish. In the tale "About the Girl Masha," Baba Yaga plays blind man's buff with two girls, three times with each one. This game is part of the trials that the heroine has to successfully overcome in order to be rewarded with gold, which is equated with happiness.[14] This story is an example of the phenomenon whereby, with time and change in social circumstances, ancient rituals were often converted into children's games. Propp suggests that Baba Yaga is blind, as she recognizes human beings by their scent ("the Russian scent"), and that symbolic and temporary blindness was practiced during initiation. For example, in "Vasilisa the Fair," Baba Yaga exclaims: "I smell Russian flesh! Who is here?" (Alexander 145) and in "Finist, the Bright Falcon," she snorts: "Tfu, tfu! I smell a human!" (*Baśnie* 41). In addition, there is reciprocal invisibility between the world of the living and that of the dead (Propp, *Raíces* 99, 101–102). According to Boris Uspienskij, the goddess Mokosh, transformed into the Christian saint Paraskeva Piatnitsa (Friday), used to punish with blindness those who trespassed the prohibition of spinning, plowing, and possibly having sex on Fridays.[15] In Polish, there is also the term *babie lato* ("baba's summer"), meaning "Indian summer" or almost invisible air threads. This expression makes sense when we remember that Baba Yaga had dominion over the weather and atmospheric phenomena and that she was connected to the invisible realm of the dead. In addition, many mountaintops in Poland, Slovakia, Slovenia, the Czech Republic, and Germany include the word "baba." Examples are the Polish Babia Góra or Babiec in the Góry Świętokrzyskie mountain range, known for its witches' Sabbaths, and Babengerg in Germany. Other telling names of places in Poland, such as Babi Jar ("Baba's Ravine") and Babie Łono ("Baba's Bosom or Womb"), also derive from "baba." Moreover, in Pole's Ukraine, the Pleiades, as well as an autumn funeral feast, may be called "Baby" (plural of "Baba") (Johns 9). In Poland and Byelorussia, this feast that connects the living with the dead is called "Dziady" or "Forefathers," a masculine form corresponding to "Baby." During this celebration, people used to place food and candles on graves, in a similar way that it is still practiced in many world cultures, such as the Aztec and Mayan. Numerous scholars also agree that "baba" is an indigenous Russian, Byelorussian, Ukrainian, Bulgarian, and Upper Sorbian name for "pelican" (Shapiro 113). The stork, a water-bird related to the pelican, is associated with fertility and, to this day in most Indo-European countries, is believed to bring babies. Interestingly, in AD 1096–1101 Catalonian *Tapís de la creació* (Tapestry of creation; figure 1.2), currently located in the Girona Cathedral, the Holy Spirit is portrayed as an aquatic bird hovering over the waters. According to Szyjewski, *wiły*, today considered female demons with long hair, connected to death, are believed to have the ability to fly on dragons or change into water birds (174). In addition, in a dialogue from a Native Canadian myth collected in the nineteenth century by Franz Boas, the hero

Figure 1.2 *Tapís de la creació* (Tapestry of creation), Girona Cathedral, Spain. Photo by author

noticed a house standing in a prairie. Pelican lived there, and asked him, "Where do you want to go?" He replied: "I am searching for my dead wife." "That is a very hard task, my grandson," said Pelican. "Only the dead can find this way easily. The living can get to the land of the dead only at great risk." Pelican gave the man a magic substance in order to help him in his quest and taught him how to use it. (127)

This has an uncanny resemblance to the context in which Baba Yaga and her hut appear in Slavic tales, collected in the nineteenth century by Aleksandr Afanas'ev. Her house also stands on the outskirts of human civilization, and she is the guardian oft hepa ssagebe tweenw orlds.

The Bird Goddess

The earlier information from the Americas reinforces the notion of the Old European veneration of the Bird Goddess, more precisely a phallic Bird Goddess, a water-bird divinity, represented by figurines that dominate from the seventh to sixth millennia BC in the Aegean and the Balkan area. This divinity is a fusion of two aspects of the Old European pantheon—the snake goddess and the bird goddess.[16] In fact, the bird was an important symbol of the goddess already in the Paleolithic era. Baba Yaga's appearance resembles a bird in several ways[17]—from her long beak-like nose with which she rakes the coals in the oven ("Sat Baba Yaga, Bony Leg, her breasts hanging over a rod, she was raking the coals with her nose, sweeping the stove with her tongue"),[18] to her abode on birds' feet, and her disheveled hair that resembles plumes. Her "bony leg" can also be a vestige of her avian nature. This resemblance points to the ancient origin of the Baba Yaga persona. In addition, Gimbutas reports that already in the Upper Paleolithic the goddess had two primary aspects: the "Giver of All" and the "Taker of All," equated with death, metamorphosis, and regeneration. The life-taking aspect was often symbolized by vultures and owls ("Women and Culture" 27–29). I further discuss these aspects in chapter 3 in relation to the pan-African Ìyàmi Òṣòròngà. There was also an ancient belief that the souls of the deceased became birds, specifically doves, and that this soul's essence was female (Bayley 2: 301; Walker, *Dictionary* 400). In many Russian tales, such as "Tale about Elena, the Wise" and "The Sea Tzar and Vasilisa the Wise," female doves have the ability to transform themselves into maidens and vice versa (*Baśnie* 51, 126–27). Ancient Slavs and Celts believed that the immortal soul survived the body and was associated with flying in the form of a bird, a butterfly, or a snake (Kravchenko 33). In numerous world traditions, divine women, such as the Greek Aphrodite and the Carthaginian Tanit, appear accompanied by birds that symbolize the sacred feminine. These notions were transformed and adapted to Christianity, where the Holy Spirit started to be portrayed as a dove. Nevertheless, in many paintings we can see that this central place of the Holy Trinity is still occupied by the Virgin Mary, Mother of God, above whom the dove as the

Holy Spirit can be seen (Oleszkiewicz-Peralba, *Black Madonna* 67). Examples are the famous Diego Velázquez painting "Feast of the Blessed Virgin Mary, Queen of Heaven," and the seventeenth- to eighteenth-century Mexican anonymous "Image of the Virgin of Guadalupe, Crowned by the Most Holy Trinity and Adornded by Saint John in Patmos and Jacob's Ladder." In literature as well, the Virgin Mary is sometimes addressed as "the dove that for eternity [was] called from the sky" (Cervantes Bk. 3 Ch. 5, Fol. 139r: 73–74).

The Serpent, the Dragon, and the Life-Death Threshold

Another remarkably important element of ancient worship is the serpent or snake figure that, similarly to Baba Yaga, also traverses worlds. *Ahi* is the Sanskrit name for it. *Echis* and *angie* are Greek and Lithuanian denominations, respectively. This would suggest that the name Baba Yaga means "Woman Snake," Yegi Baba "Snake Woman," and Yaga Yagishna "Snake of Snakes" (Kravchenko 203). Considering that the snake and the dragon were prehistoric symbols of Mother Earth and her renewal, here we find the connection between Baba Yaga and the primordial Mother Goddess in her aspect of death and regeneration. In fact, the serpent represents the earth and the underworld, the realm of the chthonian goddess. Moreover, in an incantation against the snake, recorded as late as the eighteenth century, the snake was called *Iaga zmeia bura* or "Yaga the brown snake" (Johns 28). The identification of the snake with the earth becomes clear when we realize that both words are almost exactly the same in many Slavic languages, for example, *zemlia/zmeia* in Russian and *ziemia/żmija* in Polish, respectively. In addition, *zmei/żmij* or masculine for *zmeia/żmija* is the mythological Slavic word for "dragon." The snake has been venerated in many world cultures because of its unusual qualities. Like the bird, it is an animal that dwells in several realms, namely, the earth and the underworld. Birds dwell on the earth and in the heavens and aquatic birds can also be seen as having a connection with the underworld and therefore were the most revered. The serpent, "as a surrogate of the moon, the ruler of all waters" (Briffault 2: 673), is capable of transformation. By shedding its skin every year and renewing itself, it was an ancient symbol of immortality. The snake has been long admired for its wisdom and has been used as a symbol for the medical profession, which today is still expressed in the caduceus or two intertwined serpents. According to Joseph Campbell, "the...association of the serpent is with physical and spiritual health" (286). As a consequence, we can find that the snake was connected to the goddess in many different cultures, exemplified by the Minoan Snake Goddess, the Greek Gorgon/ Medusa, the Hindu Guhyakālī and Ma Mansa Devī, and the Aztec Ciuacoatl or "Snake Woman," all identified with both destruction and regeneration. According to Marija Gimbutas:

> Perhaps because of the snake-shaped neck of the swan, crane, stork, and goose and their periodic renewal each spring after they have spent the winter months in the south, the symbolism of the bird is interwoven with that of the snake. Both are incarnate of life energy and are the seats of the souls of the dead. The Snake and the Bird Goddesses are guardians (genii, penates) of the family, clan, and later in history, of the city (as Athena of Athens, whose symbols are bird and snake). They oversee the continuity of life energy, the well-being and health of the family, and the increase of the food supply. (*Language*317) [19]

In addition, Lithuanian-born scholar Marija Gimbutas emphasized the traditional importance of the house snake in Lithuania, which still in the twentieth century was considered the protector of the household and was fed milk.[20] Similarly, Byelorussians, Ukrainians, and Czechs had great respect for the house snake that lived behind the stove (Kravchenko 33–34). Moreover, in Bulgaria, "[t]he snake is seen as the guardian of the home and the fields, and also as a symbol of immortality and fertility" (MacDermott 213). The snake was the protector of the household, the link between the living and the dead. In Baba Yaga's hut, the serpent is represented by the pipe of the oven, which in Russia was called "snake" (Hubbs 46). Many Slavic and Baltic legends, such as the Lithuanian "Eglė žalčių karalienė" ("The Queen of the Snakes"; Miłosz 91–98) and the Polish "O wężowej wdzięczności" ("About Snake's Gratitude"; Wortman 123–30), reflect the importance of serpents in these ancient cultures. In today's Lithuania, sculptures representing crowned snakes, which reflect ancient legends and tales, are still a frequent sight in public places. Szyjewski reports that among Western and Southern Slavs this ruler of the otherworld appears as a crowned snake guarding golden treasures under the name of "King of Snakes" (Poland), "Snake/Zmei Tsar" (Serbia), and "Money Snake/Zmei" (Lusatia) (58). A two-headed eagle, resembling two intertwined serpents, still is the national emblem of Germany, Albania, and Russia. Moreover, in the Greek Orthodox Church, the emblem of the authority of the bishop was a staff headed by two serpents.

The serpent and its mythical equivalent, the dragon, appears in myth as the guardian of the Waters of Life (Briffault 2: 670, 673). Quetzalcoatl (figure 1.3), the feathered serpent or dragon, was the great civilizing god of the Aztecs and other Mesoamerican peoples. In addition, the *zmiei* or "dragon," who frequently appears in Slavic and European fairy tales as the antagonist, is the guardian of the boundary to the other world—the realm of the dead—and can be considered Baba Yaga's alter ego (Kravchenko 210). He guards the frontier between the two realms, separated by the river of fire, at the Kalinovyi, or "snowball tree-wood" bridge. Interestingly, this tree, *viburnum opulus*, produces flowers that look like balls of yarn[21]—possibly another connection with the all-powerful goddess figure who spins the thread of life and decides about the life-death passage. The dragon's characteristics, a combination of snake and bird that echo the Bird and Snake Goddess, portray him as encompassing all three realms—the earth, the heavens, and the underworld—making him all-powerful. The dragon

Figure 1.3 The Mesoamerican feathered serpent, Quetzalcoatl, Mexico City. Photo by author

can also include other animals, such as the lizard, the panther, the lion, and the he-goat.²² A related mythological figure is the griffin, usually portrayed with the head, front legs, and wings of a bird, the body of a lion, and the long tail of a serpent, alluding to the three realms as well. Because of its extraordinary abilities, the dragon is revered in many cultures, such as the Egyptian, the Babylonian, the ancient Indian, the Greek, the Aztec, and the Chinese. According to Propp, it appears with the formation of a caste state and the introduction of anthropomorphic gods (*Raíces* 328, 361). The dragon in the tales flies on wings of fire and usually has three, six, nine, or twelve heads; it can emerge from the sea, forest, or a mountain cavern. This monster is also an alter ego of Koshchei Bessmertnyi ("Koshchei the Deathless") and of *wikhr* ("whirlwind") of the tales (Kravchenko 205, 225), as well as of Baba Yaga. The dragon or *zmiei* is the mythological representation of the serpent and embodies the monster of the chaos that destroys the cosmic order. The meaning of the *zmiei* of fire is similar to that of the River of Fire from the tales, which represents the threshold between the realm of the living and of the dead, called *Nav'* in Proto-Slavic and *Nawie* in

Polish (Szyjewski 78). As the dragon, Baba Yaga lives "[a]t the very end of the world, in the farthest kingdom, behind the river of fire" (*Baśnie* 78), and her specialty is the transition between the world of the living and that of the dead. In Bulgaria, *zmiei*, which could be male or female (*zmieitsa*), was seen as the guardian protector of the whole community (MacDermott 65–66). Originally, in Europe and Asia, the dragon was portrayed as a positive donor, but with time it evolved into its opposite. According to Propp, this was due to the fact that its original form started to contradict new forms of civilization and society (*Raíces* 335, 340). For example, with the advent of Christianity, the formerly holy snake and dragon figures were demonized and started to be portrayed as the causes of evil, stepped upon by the Virgin Mary and other saints.[23] According to the biblical story, the serpent caused the fall of Eve and the loss of Paradise, and the dragon was represented as a horrible monster, often with seven heads, as in Revelation.

Sacred Colors, Helpers, and Horses

In the tales, the goddess-witch Baba Yaga is in possession of many magical objects, such as mirrors, votive towels, scarves, combs, rings, and balls of yarn, that she gives to women to help them find a mate and procreate, thus fulfilling her generative function in the wheel of life. These sacred objects bridge spiritual and material realms and give their possessor control of existence (Washington 20). As she controls nature, in the tales Baba Yaga has many servants from the plant, animal, human, and cosmic realm, including air, water, wind, rain, the sun, and the moon. Her special helpers are three riders, as portrayed in "Vasilisa the Fair." The white one represents dawn, the red one the sun, and the black one the night. Interestingly, in Polish incantations, there appear three female *zorze* or "auroras": Utrenica, Południca, and Wieczornica, which correspond to dawn, midday, and evening, representing transformation (Szyjewski 71). Similar to Slavic "auroras," in pan-African belief systems, it is considered that the ancient Mothers have control over terrestrial and spiritual worlds as well as over sacred and linear time. They are:

> Ambassadors of the sun;
> Ambassadors of the afternoon;
> Ambassadors of the night;
> A composed collective, they [we] meet Àwọn Ìyàmi.
> "Ìtàn-Oríkì Ìyàmi Òṣòròngà"[24]

According to Turner, there is an almost universal meaning to the colors white, red, and black. White often represents purity and fertility; red, life and power; and black, decomposition and death. They correspond to certain bodily fluids: whiteness to semen and milk, redness to blood, and blackness to feces and products of bodily decay. In this way, the human body may be considered a microcosm of the universe.[25] These three sacred colors also reflect the notions of consciousness, action, and lack of consciousness or chaos. According to the Chhandogya Upanishad from ancient Hinduism, "The red colour of (gross) fire is the colour of (the original fire); the white colour of (gross) fire is the colour of the original water...; the black colour of (gross) fire is the colour of (the original earth)...the three colours (forms) alone are true."[26] These colors correspond to the three *gunas* or "strands" of existence (a metaphor taken from weaving) that permeate all nature or *praktri*. They are called *sattwa, rajas,* and *tamas.* "Sattwa is the quality of purity and tranquility (and may be equated with white); *rajas* is the active principle which initiates *karma* (and may be equated with red), while *tamas* is 'constrictive, obstructive, and conductive to lethargic apathy (and may be equated with black).'"[27] They are related to the passage of time and regeneration, and they also symbolize the virgin, the mother, and the crone aspects of the goddess. Turner believes that the significance of the three colors comes from a remote, pre-Indo-European past (*Forest* 86). A related custom exists to this day among Southern Slavs. Every first of March, Bulgarians and Macedonians still exchange small female, with sometimes connected male, figures made of white and red thread twisted together, called Baba Marta or Martenitsa, at times reduced to interwoven white and red threads[28] (figure 1.4). People, animals, and tools are decorated with them. They are believed to ward off evil and bring good fortune and health. This ritual is related to the personification of the month March in the figure of Baba Marta ("Granny March") as an elderly, powerful, and ambivalent lady with a changing temper reflected in the weather, and to spring cleaning. In another popular version, women and children wear Martenitsas until they see a stork, at which point they attach them to trees for fertility and good health. The mythical Baba Marta is possibly a remnant of an ancient belief system and the honor given to a real-life baba ("midwife") (MacDermott 187–91). Her old age, changeability, and magical powers over -fertility and the weather remind us of Baba Yaga.

As mentioned earlier, the horse as well as the bird were sacred totemic animals already in the Paleolithic. Therefore, it is not

Figure 1.4 Contemporary Bulgarian Martenitsas. Author's collection and photo

surprising that Baba Yaga's horses are also winged and magical. As a horse goddess, she can give presents, such as the firebreathing flying horse, to male youths that please her (Hubbs 39). For example, in the tale "Maria Morevna," Ivan gets from Baba Yaga a "wonderful horse that flies like a bird" (*Baśnie* 81). According to Propp, the horse substituted the bird in Eurasia, and its Russian name, *losad*, also meant *ptiza* or "bird" in prehistoric times. An analogous situation occurred on the American continent with the magical bear, which was also supplanted by the horse (*Raíces* 247–48). In Slavic areas, the bear was a mediator who was believed to "die" in the winter and be "reborn" in the spring. The dates of the "falling asleep" of the bear (November 30) and of his "waking up" (March 25) were converted into the Christian holidays of Saint Andrew and of the Annunciation of Our Lady, respectively (Szyjewski 180). In Slavic fairy tales, horses are represented flying with their riders-helpers on them, and in some tales there is still the image of the hero flying on a bird. This representation has persisted in the collective subconscious to the present day; for example, it is prominently featured in the 2009 3D movie *Avatar*, in which animals, especially birds, are the hero's helpers. The white horse of the tales represents the dawn and is linked to the land of death, or of incorporeal beings. Sometimes it is silver, bluish, or invisible. In Revelation, the beast rides a white horse (La Biblia, Apocalipsis 19.11). The red horse represents noon, the sun, and fire. In the Vedic religion of India, there existed the cult of fire and the horse, incarnated in the god Agni, represented as a firehorse. This horse was an intermediary between realms. In the Middle Ages, the Christian Devil, also connected to fire, was an intermediary (Propp, *Raíces* 252–62). In African and African-derived religions, this mediator is the trickster god Exu as well as his female counterpart, Pombagira, in Brazil, discussed in chapter 3. The black-winged horse is the night rider. The entities converted into demons after Christianization had mediating qualities and were connected to the air, the forest, the water, the fields, and the household. Slavic examples are Baba Yaga,

Domownik, Nawki, and Rusałki (Szyjewski 158–59, 162). In the "Tale about Elena, the Wise," the devil is described as a trickster who helps the protagonist (*Baśnie* 49–55). Similarly to Baba Yaga and the triune goddess in general, the horses are connected to the passage of time and transformation. It is remarkable how in the magical tales the essence of the ancient sacred elements, such as the bird, the horse, and the three colors, was preserved, even though on the surface their significance was camouflaged, or simply forgotten.

As in many other cultures on all continents, in Slavic lands the goddess was portrayed as a trinity denoted by the maiden (Rusałka, usually used in plural as "Rusałki"), the mother (Mother Moist Earth), and the crone (Baba Yaga), represented by the aforementioned three sacred colors. In Yoruba- and Bantu-derived Afro-Latin American syncretic religions, such as the Brazilian Candomblé and the Cuban Regla de Ocha (Santería), the correspondent figures worshipped to this day are Oxum (Ochún), Iemanjá (Yemayá), and Nanã (Naná Burukú). In the Native Mexican Aztec religion, parallel deities were Xochiquetzal ("Flowery Quetzal Flower"), Tonantzin ("Our Mother"), and Toci ("Our Grandmother"). Toci was also called Tlalli yiollo ("Heart of the Earth") and Grandmother of the Baths (Sahagún, Bk. 1: 4).

In the magical tales, Baba Yaga also has a pair of independent hands awaiting her orders, and the sorcerer Koshchey Bessmertnyi, related to the destructive powers of nature. As it can be deduced from the earlier discussion, Baba Yaga used to be a powerful goddess, with dominion over life and death and the three spheres of nature—the subterranean, the earthly, and the heavenly, so that in olden times the weather, fertility, crops, and health depended on her, and she was therefore much respected and feared by the peasants. This aspect of the mighty Baba Yaga is presented in Isaac Bashevis Singer's novel *The King of the Fields*, which recounts the legendary times when the inhabitants of the Polish lands were in the process of transformation from the nomadic lifestyle of hunters-gatherers to that of an agricultural society of the Neolithic era. Baba Yaga also appears in his *Stories for Children*, particularly "Joseph and Koza," where she represents the evil powers that were overcome with the more "civilized" forces of Christianity in the ninth–tenth centuries AD. In this story, she is portrayed as an evil witch, with male and female characteristics, who demands human sacrifice. As seen in the magical tales, together with her young maiden aspect—the Rusałka—Baba Yaga survived the transitions from hunting-gathering to horticultural, farming, and herding economies. As the goddess of hunters, she was represented by the bird and as one of warriors and herders by the horse. She was the initiator of women, as well as men, into the female world of fertility (Hubbs 43). Baba Yaga was also associated with the frog as a "wandering uterus."[29] For example, in the Polish tale "O królewnie zaklętej w żabę" ("About a Princess Bewitched into a Frog," Gliński 38–47), Baba Yaga helps a young prince to acquire a frog-bride who in reality is an enchanted princess (Oleszkiewicz-Peralba, *Black Madonna* 24). In the Russian tale "Go There I Know Not Where, Fetch That I Know Not What," the only being who can lead the hero across the Flaming River is an Old Frog who is addressed as "Mother" and can change in size; she has lived in a marsh for hundreds of years (Alexander 193–95). In Lithuania, the toad (*rupūžė*) is still believed to be linked to death, healing, and regeneration (Gimbutas, *Living Goddesses* 207). As discussed earlier, other Baba Yaga's associations are with the bear as the caretaker of forest, as in "King Bear" (Afanas'ev 393–98), and with the serpent and the dragon as self-renovating beings connected to several spheres.

Womb and Tomb: The Initiation Hut, the Oven, and the Mortar

An important element of Slavic fairy tales, linked to Baba Yaga, is the hut on hens' feet. Potebnja considers that the hut is Baba Yaga herself, as she fills it completely with her body.[30] According to descriptions in different tales, collected in the eighteenth and in the twentieth centuries:

> Yagaia Baba was lying there, her legs stretched from corner to corner. Her iron nose was sticking into the ceiling, her breasts were hanging over rods, and her little children were suckling... Her feet were on the threshold, her lips on the roof-pillar, her arms stretched from corner to corner, her nose in the ceiling
> ...her nose was on the oven, her eyes on a shelf above it, she was dragging pots around with her lips, and raking the oven with her tongue. (Johns 157, 160)

Similarly, in Afanas'ev's "Finist, the Bright Falcon," Baba Yaga Bony Leg: "with her legs reaches from wall to wall, hangs her lips outside the window, and her nose got adhered to the ceiling" (*Baśnie* 41). In this way, the hut, filled up by Baba Yaga's body, resembles both a womb and a coffin, elements emphasized by Turner as characteristic of liminal personae (*Forest* 99) and places where transformations occur. It also echoes Neolithic burials where corpses were placed on wooden platforms above the ground, as described earlier. In addition, the earth was considered to be the sacred womb and the tomb, as it gives life to all living things and receives them at death. In Paleolithic burials, the dead were placed in the earth in an embryonic position and were covered with ochre red or hematite to magically provoke their rebirth (Szafrański 62–63). Interestingly, seventh- and sixth-millenia BC temples were conceived as the body or house of the goddess (Gimbutas, "Women and Culture" 25), and many contemporary sanctuaries and representations of the Virgin Mary, heir of Mother Earth, are still placed in grottos. The hut of the tales stands on fowls' feet (*kurie nogi*), and it is filled up by Baba Yaga, who either lies or sits on the earthen floor, on a bench, or on the stove. On other occasions, she flies. She is never portrayed walking. Originally, the hut was probably an animal or had the shape of a bird,[31] as in the bird-shaped temples found and described by Marija Gimbutas in *The Goddesses and Gods of Old Europe* (67). This transition hut, located far from inhabited areas, has no windows and stands facing the forest and is away from the hero. In order to enter, he has to pronounce a magical formula, such as: "Little hut, little hut! Turn your front to us and your back to the forest" or "Little hut, little hut, stand as you did before, as mother placed you, with your back to the forest and with your front to me,"[32] and the hut turns around to face him. Propp contends that in ancient Skandinavia, the entrances to houses were never at the north side, since this position represented the entrance to the world of death. The fact that in some tales the hut spins by itself and stands on a spindle, on ram's horns, or on animal legs is a modification of the original myths. The hut did not spin by itself; the hero had to make it turn with a magical formula (*Raíces* 81, 179). In the hut, the hero is assigned different trials he has to overcome in order to achieve his goal—usually finding the princess and marrying her. Similarly, during ancient initiation rituals, a youth was subjected to a series of testing hardships before being considered an adult.

As discussed earlier, similar to the great Mother Goddess of life and death, Baba Yaga is the ancient mistress of animals and the forest (*khoziaika lesa*) and the guardian of the land of the dead and her dwelling can be regarded as an initiation hut. Baba Yaga is also strongly linked to bone remains, as exemplified in the many elements surrounding her hut and her "bony leg" (*kostianaia noga*). In his article "Khettskaia ^{SAL}ŠU.GI i slavianskaia Baba-Yaga," Toporov relates Baba Yaga to ^{SAL}ŠU.GI, the wise woman and mistress of funeral ceremonies from the Hittite religion who helps the deceased enter into the land of the dead. They are both of old age and play a role in cremation rituals with roots in ancient pre-Indo-European tradition. According to Toporov, the *skazka* featuring Baba Yaga not only reflects the death theme in general, but also the burial ritual itself, which was accompanied by the burning of the body, and the bones may suggest the ritual keeping of bone remains (32, 34). The hero's wanderings symbolize the journey of the soul after death. Baba Yaga's connection to cremation practices links her to such

Indian goddesses as Kālī and Dhūmāvatī. It seems that among Eastern Slavs, there were two superimposed burial rituals: the first—burial in the earth as the Cosmic Mother, performed in a fetal position, and the second—cremation, connected to the heavens and the god Perun (Szyjewski 204). The dichotomy of earth and sky would suggest that the first was of pre-Indo-European origin, corresponding to Old Europe's matrilineal culture, and the second developed with the Indo-European invasions of nomadic warriors from the Eastern steppes, and the change to pastoral economy starting in the third millenium BC. Nevertheless, as Szafrański attests, later a mixed earth and cremation burial was practiced by burying the ashes in the earth (145–46).

The focal point of Baba Yaga's hut is the oven, an instrument of both destruction and creation. Like the womb, it holds the secret of fertility and generation and like the tomb, it connects Baba Yaga to the underworld and the ancestors. The magical oven, where it was believed the ancestors resided, was the most important place in the household. In the tale "Chestnut Grey," Ivan the Fool, who repeatedly goes to see his dead father, feeds him and receives his help, usually lays on a stove eating mushrooms he collected in the forest (Alexander 133–40). Mushrooms are strongly connected to the earth and the ancestors, as half of their body is constituted by their root, and they have magical properties. Several species can provoke altered states of consciousness, sickness, and even death, and today they are still used as mediators in Native American rituals. Baba Yaga repeatedly tries to place children in her oven. This action may be linked to ritual burning and roasting of neophytes during initiation ceremonies, which corresponded to similar actions performed with the dead (Propp, *Raíces* 75, 158). This was due to the fact that it was believed that during initiation, the youth descended to the realm of death, and the ritual itself was considered a temporary death. Various scholars agree that the action of burning in the magical tales, commonly interpreted as malevolent, is also related to Russian, Ukrainian,

Byelorussian, and Siberian tradition of "baking" of children (*perepekanie*) in order to eliminate their sickness (Johns 95; Kravchenko 192). A similar custom was related to the mortar and the ritual "grinding" of children for the same purpose.[33] Therefore, what was used for ritual and healing was reinterpreted, and often reverted, in the tales. For example, in the tale "Baba Yaga and the Brave Youth" (Afanas'ev 76–79), the hero outsmarts the witch and shoves Baba Yaga and her daughter into the oven instead. Nonetheless, the oven was the most important place around which the traditional household was built. It was the site of transformation and connected the living with the ancestors.

Baba Yaga's hut, the oven, and the mortar are also representative of the womb and of the mother. The mortar and pestle are instruments of change—both creation and destruction—as they are used to grind grain and prepare flax for spinning; symbolically, they correspond to the womb and the phallus that start the cycle of generation, birth, nurture, and death. Baba Yaga is famous for cooking and for spinning, activities associated with the feminine realm and symbolic of life generation and transformation. Her thread, which spans different worlds, is made of bones and entrails of the dead (Hubbs 38–39). An analogy can be found in regard to the pan-African Mothers, Àwọn Ìyá Wa, who are believed to control and hold elongated objects, such as long livers, umbilical cords, amnions, clothes for wrapping children on one's back, and head ties (Washington 19), that may be seen as connectors to the origins and as intermediaries between the human and the spiritual realms. During his initiation, the hero of the tales has to enter Baba Yaga's hut, a frightening place positioned in a liminal space between nature and civilization and between the world of the living and of the dead, in order to symbolically die and be reborn, transformed into a man. The hut stands in the dense, enchanted forest (*v dremuchim lesu*), a marginal and dangerous place on the outskirts of the village. The birch tree, abundant in North-Eastern Europe, represented beginnings and birth, and its white bark was probably connected to the White Goddess, both birth-giver and death-bringer (Walker, *Dictionary* 461). The birch is the most holy of trees in Russia and represents the female divinity. It symbolizes the axis mundi, with its crown in the skies, the realm of celestial bodies; its trunk on earth, the realm of mortals; and its roots in the underworld, the realm of the dead. It also represents human life—birth, marriage, death—and is connected to beginnings, marriage, power, and purification (Kopaliński 34–35).

The hut in the forest is a threshold to another world. In fact, the origin of the word "liminality" can be found in the Latin words *limes* ("limit") and *limen* ("*threshold*"). This entry to the realm of the dead can only be surmounted through the hut (Propp, *Raíces* 79). Inside, the hero is submitted to interrogation, but first he requests food, drink, a bath, and a bed to rest, which are conceded by the donor Baba Yaga. For example, in the "Tale about the Apples of Youth and the Water of Life," Baba Yaga "[f]ed [Prince Ivan], gave him to drink, and laid him in bed. She sat at his bedside and started to question him" (*Baśnie* 147). As the hero of the tales is submitted to a number of difficult and dangerous tasks, during the ancient ritual of initiation a prepuberty boy was submitted to a number of hardships, including physical torture and mutilation (amputation of a finger), circumcision, scarring, symbolic burning and roasting, as well as a long instruction on the secrets of hunting, social norms and customs, religious secrets, and everything necessary for life. It was believed that the initiate underwent a temporary death, after which he resurrected as a new man. These initiation practices provoked temporary madness and amnesia (Propp, *Raíces* 74–75). Initiations in a dark forest or in a special hut are still being practiced in different cultures. An example is the *casa de força* ("house of strength"), initiation hut of the Afro-Brazilian religion Candomblé, where aspirants (*abião*) have to spend three weeks to three months without leaving or communicating with the outside world, while participating in a number of rituals in order to be cleansed, instructed, and born again into their new religion.[34] The fact that in the tales Baba Yaga consistently comments on the "Russian scent" can be explained by the circumstance that she belongs to the world of the dead and notices the living for their scent, since the dead and the living are not visible to each other. Again, this constitutes a reversal of the real life situation where the scent of the dead is repugnant to the living (Propp, *Raíces* 88–89). This interpretation is consistent with the Native Canadian tale "The Dead Woman," where a man looking for his dead wife reaches the underground house of a chief, who at first "wanted to devour the man, but when he got closer to him, he cried out, 'He stinks; he isn't dead yet!'" (Boas 127).

From Matriarchal Goddess to Contemporary Witch

By her actions of spinning, weaving, baking, and feeding, Baba Yaga is connected to the traditional feminine realm, similarly to the Finno-Slavic goddess Mokosh and her heir, the Christian Saint Paraskeva-Piatnitsa. Nevertheless, she is also called *ved'ma* (Russ.) and *wiedźma* (Pol.), which today means "witch." A look at the etymology of this world is most revealing. We can see that it comes from the Russian *vedunya* ("the woman who knows"), *vedomaya zhena* ("wise woman") (Kravchenko 53), and *ved'ma* ("the one who knows"), as *vedat'* means "to know." Similarly, in Polish, *wiedźma* or "witch" comes from "the woman who knows," and *wiedzieć* is "to know." We can observe how these important feminine figures have been demonized, coming to represent the opposite of their original meaning. Interestingly, the same semantic transformation did not occur with the Russian masculine form of this word, *vedun*. Similarly, Washington reports that after the imposition of Christianity and Islam, the Yoruban powerful Mothers, the Ajé, discussed in chapter 3, started to be identified as "witches," while their male counterparts, the Oṣó, retained their respectability as "wizards" (32, 291). In addition, related words are the Polish masculine form *wieszcz*/veshch/, the feminine *wieszczka*/veshchka/, as well as the Russian masculine *veshchun* and the feminine *veshchunia*, meaning "seer," "diviner," or "soothsayer." According to the *Mahānirvāna Tantra*, the Tantric word for a sacred harlot, attendant Devī of one of the Mahāvidyās in India, was *veshya* (Ch. 13: 328). These prostitute-priestesses were the embodiment of beauty and kindness (*charis* or *caritas*—"charity"), "mother-love, tenderness, comfort, mystical enlightenment, and sex," and "dispensed the grace of the Goddess" in Hindu, Middle Eastern, and Mediterranean temples, among others. "Veshya" is also the possible origin of Hestia or Vesta, the oldest goddess names in Greece and Rome.[35] The Polish *wieszczka*/veshchka/ and the Russian *veshchunia* are even closer phonetic matches for "veshya" and suggest that they all had divine functions and were highly regarded.

The etymology of these Polish and Russian names is consistent with the fact that women were traditionally the bearers of sacred knowledge. They escorted the dead to the other world, and their assistance, both practical and ceremonial, was of utmost importance during birth and marriage as well. They were the primary healers and fortune-tellers of the community (Kravchenko 57–58). Unfortunately, these powerful roles may have also been the reason why women who performed them became demonized, persecuted, and burnt at the stake as witches, and their functions were taken up by men. For example, Siberian male shamans often use feminine clothing and attributes, such as iron circles for breasts and braided hair. They also have privileges customarily given to women but forbidden to men, such as entering the room of the mother for three days after giving birth to a child. Moreover, a woman shaman is called *utugan*, a word connected to Mongolian *Etugen* or Earth Goddess (*Etugen-eke*—"Mother-Earth"). As a consequence, many scholars believe that originally only female shamans existed and the male shaman supplanted the female (Czaplicka 197–99, 144, 147). Similarly, in the Indian Muṭiyēṭṭu performance, the goddess Bhadrakālī is enacted by men wearing feminine costumes adorned by snakes around the breasts and the headdress (Caldwell, *Terrifying* 144), and in the Yoruban Gẹ̀lẹ̀dẹ́ performance, the terrible ancestral mothers, the *iyá mi*, are also enacted exclusively by men, as described in chapter 3 of this book. Similarly, Western Slavic, pre-Christian holy men did not cut their hair and wore long robes (Szyjewski 153), and Yoruban priests in Africa wear women's clothing and hair dress to perform religious ceremonies.[36] In addition, in his *The Interpretation of Cultures*, Clifford Geertz describes a Balinese ritual that enacts a combat between Rangda—a witch "depicted as a wasted old widow, prostitute, and eater of infants [that] comes to spread plague and death"—and the monster Barong—"depicted as a kind of cross between a clumsy bear, a silly puppy, and a strutting Chinese dragon." The hideous and powerful Rangda, with her fangs, strings of entrails, and long red fire tongue, embodies sheer horror and death, resembling representations of the goddess Kālī, but she is still embodied by a male dancer, while Barong is a hilarious figure (114–15). In Judaism, Christianity, and Islam women became further excluded from religious posts and the performance of holy rites, which traditionally have been executed only by men; curiously, these men also wear robes.

According to Propp, with the decline of matriarchy,[37] the deity Baba Yaga lost her motherly functions, although she kept its attributes, such as large breasts, and only retained her power over animals and the dead. In the tales, she is the totemic clan ancestress and goddess of the dead, connected to fire and the stove, as well as the mistress of animals. Her chief function was trespassed to the male (*Raíces* 103–108), as it happened in Central Europe with the passage from farming to herding economy, which gave rise to private ownership and a patriarchal system. Nevertheless, vestiges of the female sovereign role are clearly visible in the "Tale about the Apples of Youth and the Water of Life," where "the Blue-Eyed Maiden, a niece of Baba Yaga's, is a strong and powerful ruler" who has 12 female warriors at her disposal and is free to exercise her sexual freedom

(*Baśnie* 142–57). In addition, remnants of matriarchal rule may still be detected in some tales. In the *skazka*, "Maria Morevna," the protagonist, is presented in the following manner:

> Maria Morevna found Prince Ivan to her liking and he married her.
> Maria Morevna, the beautiful queen, took Prince Ivan with her to her kingdom. They lived together for some time, then the queen decided to make war; she left all her household in Prince Ivan's charge and told him: "Go everywhere, take care of everything."(Afanas'ev555)

This tale, where the queen is clearly the one in charge, echoes matrilocal social organization,[38] and her portrayal corresponds to the "fighter" type of Baba Yaga. Interestingly, the name "Morevna," which means "daughter of Morena," suggests matrilineal succession.[39] In some Slavic languages, such as Russian, until today sons and daughters are called by their first name after which comes the first name of their father (*otechestvo*). For example, if Maria's father was Sergei, she would be called Maria Sergeievna. Nevertheless, this custom is currently not practiced with the mother's name. In addition, in many tales, such as "About the Silver Saucer and Juicy Apple" (*Baśnie* 15–20), it is the youngest daughter that is endowed with special talents and qualities, which suggests a remnant of a matrilineal ultimogeniture law, in which the youngest daughter in the female line was the heir (Kohli 164). Curiously, Morena (Morana, Marena, Mara, Marzanna) was the old goddess of death, winter, and nightmares. This would indicate that the beautiful Maria from the tale is also the old woman and a formidable entity, possibly the fighter aspect of Baba Yaga. In Poland, a ritual burning of Marzanna (figure 1.5) is a symbol of winter, death, darkness, and decomposition that leads to the rebirth of nature. The latter is portrayed by the ritual Maik ("Little May"), Nowe Latko ("Little New Summer"), or a rooster—a lunar fertility symbol—and is still widely performed during the spring equinox. The ritual throwing into the water of a burning figure of Marzanna or

Figure 1.5   Polish Marzanna. Photo by author

Panna Moru ("Lady of a Sudden, Collective Death") symbolizes the trespassing of a Flaming River that separates the world of the dead from the one of the living (Szyjewski 123, 133). In the cycle of tales of the "fighting Baba Yaga," she rides a horse and often leads an army of Amazons. Similarly, in the cycle of tales about the Virgin Tzardom in the sun-country, the ruler, a Virgin-Tzar, has an army of courageous women (Kohli 186–87).

Stones and Embroideries

In the magical tales, Baba Yaga is portrayed sitting or lying down on her hut's earthen floor. The Great Mother was also represented sitting on the earth, on a mountain, and later on a throne (Kravchenko 196). Related stone effigies from the first millennium AD, probably of Scynthian and Finno-Ugric origin, are called "Stone Babas"—*kamienne baby* in Polish and *kamennye baby* in Russian (Hubbs 8, 20)—and they can still be found today throughout Eurasia. These mysterious figures make sense when we consider that the earth was worshipped on mountains topped with stones, and stones were considered Mother Earth's bones (Kopaliński 139). In fact, a stone was seen as a substitute for a mountain, and Slavic enthronements were performed on stone thrones or on holy stones (Szyjewski 87–88), which earlier were identified with the goddess. Moreover, the name of the Egyptian goddess Isis means "throne." There is also a strong and ancient tradition of worshipping Mother Moist Earth and Holy Earth, among Eastern and Western Slavs, respectively. The earth was a holy persona, central of the trinity that included the Rusałka, Mother Moist Earth, and Baba Yaga. As discussed earlier, these figures represent the young maiden, the mature mother, and the crone stages of life, aspects of the goddess that are interchangeable with each other. Prayers were addressed to the earth, oaths were sworn by her, marriage rituals included the swallowing of a piece of earth, and confessions were done to the earth as the absolute judge and redeemer (Kravchenko 25–26). Moreover, in later times, pieces of the black, fertile earth were taken and cherished by exiles and emigrants to foreign lands.[40] Similarly, the pan-African Mothers, Àwon Ìyá Wa, represent Ìyá-Ayé—the Mother of the Earth—who is believed to be the ultimate judge and cosmic administrator of justice (Washington 35).

To this day, embroidered towels and garments in Russia and in Ukraine show a red figure of the goddess on a white background, flanked by plants, birds, animals, and particularly horse riders. Here we can observe the connection of the riders from the tales to the goddess figure. These motifs gradually became more geometrical, and today the goddess is often represented as a tree or a flower (figure 1.6). In addition, traditional and contemporary Polish paper cutouts still portray the goddess as the lady of the heavens, the earth, and the underworld (figure 1.7) or as the center of the flowering tree of life, which also unites these three spheres. (figure 1.8) She is accompanied by growing plants, flowers, and celestial bodies. (figure 1.9) This Cosmic

Figure 1.6 Goddess motifs on shirt embroideries, Poland, beginning of the twentieth century. Photo by author

Figure 1.7 The goddess as the Lady of the Heavens, the Earth, and the Underworld, paper cutout, Poland. Author's collection

Figure 1.8 The goddess as the tree of life, paper cutout, Poland. Author's collection

Figure 1.9 The goddess accompanied by growing plants, flowers, and celestial bodies, paper cutout, Łowicz region, Poland, beginning of the twentieth century. Photo by author

Three is also the axis mundi, which started all creation. In Polish popular art, one of the most frequent motifs is that of two birds seated on the branches of a tree. (figure 1.10) In traditional belief, they represent the two creators of the world—God and the Devil. In a Karpatian mountains Christmas Carol, which still keeps the ancient elements of a cosmological myth, the cosmic creators are presented as two doves sitting on an oak tree. They converse in the following manner:

> Two doves on an oak tree
> Deliberated in this way,
> ....
> How are we to create the world?

The bird and the reptilian god's helpers were later transformed into god's servants, and ultimately—into his enemies (Szyjewski 30, 37; Szafrański221).

Figure 1.10 Two birds on a tree, paper cutout, Poland. Author's collection

All-encompassing mother figures of Northern and Central Europe were the Finno-Slavic goddess Mokosh and the Slavic Złota Baba ("Golden Woman"). This deity was also called the goddess Żywa /Zhiva/ ("Alive") or Żywie/Zhivie/ in Poland (figure 1.11). Her other names included Zajęta Języ Baba, Baba Jędza, and Baba Jaga (Perkowska 22). Her heir, and a transition figure between paganism and Christianity, in Russia, Ukraine, Serbia, Bulgaria, and Macedonia, was Saint Paraskeva Piatnitsa. In opposition to "the Most Pure" Virgin Mary, she was called "the Dirty One," was connected to moisture and fertility, and was portrayed spinning next to a well of water (Hubbs 116–17).

Figure 1.11 The goddess Żywa accompanied by growing plants, paper cutout, Łowicz region, Poland, end of the nineteenth century. Photo by author

Paraskeva's picture was often paired with that of the Virgin Mary, on the other side, and placed near water wells (Ivanov and Toporov 192–93), feminine symbols of fertility.

As bird goddess, Baba Yaga was presumably mighty, all knowing, all seeing, and dual, both terrifying and a wise helper. She degenerated into a goddess of the underworld, of witchcraft and misfortune, possibly with the change of the economy from farming to herding, and the advent of the Indo-European male sky gods from the Eurasian steppes, such as Perun (god of thunder and lightning), Svarog (representing the daylight sky or sun), and Stribog (god of winds, *vikhr*, the "whirwind" of the tales). In fact, both Baba Yaga and Rusałka joined the demonic realm. According to L. Stomma, Baba Yaga represents "the soul of a woman dead in childbirth," and the Rusałka is "a non-baptyzed one, engaged—dead before marriage" (Szyjewski 163). The only female deity placed by Prince Vladimir of Kiev on a hill near his royal courtyard, shortly before Christianization, in AD 980, was Mokosh,[41] who later persisted in the veneration of Mother Moist Earth (Mat' Syra Zemlya) and Holy Mother Earth (Zemlya Svyata Mati). During Christianization in the ninth–tenth centuries AD, she was substituted by a new central female figure—the Mother of God or Virgin Mary. Many of the traits and powers of the Rusałka, Mother Earth, and Baba Yaga were incorporated into the Virgin Mary, called Mother of God or God Birth-Giver among Slavs. She is very miraculous, is still identified with Mother Moist Earth in Slavic Europe, and her image is often placed in grottos. Sometimes she is represented as a spinner of life. Examples are the fifteenth-century painting "Virgin Mary with a Distaff," by the Master of Erfurt, and the twelfth-century fresco from the church of Sorpe, Calatonia. Nevertheless, her chthonic, all devouring aspects and her connection to the realm of the dead, as well as the independence and sexuality of the dancing and spinning Rusałki were eliminated.

The Great Goddess Baba Yaga, as other mighty female divine figures discussed in this book, was disarmed and demonized.

She is probably the most ancient of them, going back to pre-Indo-European, Old Europe, before 3,000 BC. Therefore today, unlike the other deities, she is never worshipped, and the only remnant of her is a gruesome witch figure that appears in children's tales and folklore.

CHAPTER 2

Kālī, the Ultimate Fierce Feminine

Devoutly I call to mind Her, the Mother of the whole universe, ŚivéH erself.

—*Karpūrādi-stotra,* "Invocation" 1 7

Who can explain Your play, Mother?
What do You take, what give back?
You give and take again.

—Sen18

Kālī, the ultimate creator, preserver, and destroyer, is the epitome of the types of goddesses we are looking at in this book, in many ways the opposite of what we think of in connection with the word "woman" or "goddess." She is the primordial wilderness and chaos, the original form of all things and eternity, but also change—time, destruction, and death:

> O you who, in the form of minutes, moments and other divisions of time, bring about change in things, and have (thus) the power to destroy the universe.
>
> ....
>
> Salutation be to you, O Narayani, you who have the power of creation, sustentation and destruction and are eternal. (*Devī-māhātmyam*C h.11:9 ,11)

> She is without beginning or end,
> Whose Body is imagined to be blue of colour,
> Because like the blue sky She pervades the world...
> is imagined to be black

> Because She is colourless...
> as the Virat, the Witness of the world past, present and future
> She sees everything.
>
> (*Karpūrādi-stotra*," Prayer"44)

In Tantric belief systems, reality is seen as the result of the interaction between the male element—Śiva—and the female—Śakti—and Tantra is considered a *śākta* or Devī ("goddess") worship.[1] Such medieval Tamil literary texts as *Silapadikaram* express the śākta philosophy portraying the goddess as the supreme deity, the embodiment of wisdom adored by all gods. In fact, Śiva is described as part of Śakti, and the Brahman and Śakti are one. The goddess Kālī exists in all forms and is identified with Śakti. She is "the origin and destroyer of all things" and "the symbol of the absolute, beyond name and form, beyond individuality and specificity...[She is] the innermost essence of reality."[2]

The Ten Mahāvidyās

This ultimate truth of the universe is expressed in Tantric Hinduism and Buddhism by a group of liminal, unrestrained, and polyvalent goddesses, the Dasha Mahāvidyā ("Ten Mahāvidyās") or "Ten Great Wisdoms," that are considered to be aspects of the Great Goddess (Mahādevī), or Kālī, in which she revealed herself to Śiva (*Mahānirvāna Tantra* xxx, 47). This feminine aspect of reality is identified with knowledge and wisdom. The Mahāvidyās include Kālī, Tārā, Tripura-sundarī, Bhuvaneśvarī, Chinnamastā, Bhairavī, Dhūmāvatī, Bagalāmukhī, Mātaṅgī, and Kamalā. Their predominant characteristics are linked to death imagery, signs of decay, skulls, blood, cremation grounds, sex, wildness, outskirts, and outsiderhood. They also embody the frightening and the forbidden, as well as magical powers. They are fierce, independent, and dominant. In fact, they substantiate death, violence, pollution, and marginality, representing the opposite of what is accepted by conventional society. In addition, most of the Mahāvidyās may be considered antimodels of female behavior, often being tempestuous, enraged, domineering, and wild. In fact, according to Kinsley, their meaning has to do with subverting and mocking social norms in order to reveal the fundamental truth of the cosmos that encompasses creation, destruction, as well as constant transformation. Therefore, in order to provoke shock and awakening, their forms may be depicted in disturbing, ambiguous, contradictory, and paradoxical ways (Frawley 60). For example, Kālī, Tārā, Bhairavī, Chhinnamastā, and Dhūmāvatī are portrayed with a necklace of severed heads and Chhinnamastā as holding her own head, which she herself cut off, and drinking her own blood; in addition, several of them are depicted standing on, seated on, or having sex with supine males.

The foremost of the Mahāvidyās, usually listed in the first place, is the goddess Kālī. In fact, the other goddesses or "wisdoms" are often considered her manifestations or aspects, Tārā being especially interchangeable with Kālī. They are both untamed and explosive and represent the uncontrolled primordial, destructive power that is simultaneously purifying and transformative. Their physical aspect reflects this force. They are represented naked, with disheveled hair, wearing garlands of human heads or skulls and girdles of severed arms, and they have blood-oozing, lolling tongues; they stand on a passive body of Śiva; and they favor cremation grounds as their dwelling. They have four hands, in two of which they carry a severed head and a sword or chopper, and in the other two Tārā holds scissors and a lotus, and Kālī makes the *mudrās* of "fear not" and of dispensing boons. Kālī, like Tārā, is the epitome of a fierce, marginal goddess, who, paradoxically, dwells at the center of everything, revealing the ultimate truth. She shakes the accepted notions of reality in order to bring out the truths that humans also need to face, such as death, destruction, and horror. In order to overcome the fragmented vision of the world as reduced to opposites, such as purity-pollution, or sacred-profane, clean and unclean, left-handed Tantrism includes the ritual called *pañca tattva* or "five (forbidden) things" or "truths." In a special context and under a guru's supervision, the initiate partakes of meat, fish, wine, a paste made of parched grain (rice, barley, or wheat), and sexual intercourse with a person from a "polluted" milieu (*Mahānirvāna Tantra* 103–104), such as low caste or prostitution, in order to be woken up to the totality of universal experience.

Kālī's name is the feminine form of the Sanskrit word for "time," *kāla* being the masculine. The goddess herself represents the ravaging passage of time and death, which is another "forbidden thing." By dwelling naked on cremation grounds and engaging in the "prohibited," she confronts the devotee with original chaos and rejects human-constructed order and convention. As Kinsley contends:

> For Tantrism, she is an appropriate symbol of rituals and meditation techniques that seek to confront appropriate, and overcome forbidden, feared, "polluting" realities. As the embodiment of the polluted, feared, and loathed, she can...grant liberation, freedom from subservience to conventionality...Kālī might be taught as a symbol of ultimate reality, an embodiment of the highest truths. (*Tantric*78,90–9 1)

Therefore, Kālī's and other Mahāvidyās' highly dramatic appearances are not to be taken literally, but symbolically. Thanks to their shocking images, initiates may be shaken and the highest truths revealed to them; thus, they may achieve freedom from attachments to human thoughts and emotions.

Fragmentation and the Periphery

Kālī as well as Pombagira, Santa Muerte, and Baba Yaga represent the rejected and the periphery of their respective societies. Kālī has traditionally been worshipped by low-caste people and criminals in uncivilized and unfrequented places. She was a patron deity of the infamous Thugs and was believed to grant them magical powers. The *Bhāgavata Purāna* describes how a group of robbers ("Panis") sacrifice a son of a Brahmana sage to Bhadrakālī. The goddess explodes forth from her image in terrible rage:

In extreme wrath and indignation, her terrible face with her branch-like arched eyebrows thrown up in agitation, her dreadful, curved jaws and the movement of her blood-red eyes, showed that she was in bent on destroying this world. In terrible rage, she roared forth a thunderous laugh. Springing forward, she cut off the heads of those wicked sinners...and drank to her fill...hot wine of the blood gushing from their throats. Intoxicated with over-drinking of that blood-wine, she sang at the topmost pitch of her voice in company of her attendants, and danced and played with the ball-like lopped heads. (5.9.12–18)

An eleventh-century Tamil text, the *Kālīngattuparani* by Jayamkondar, describes her temple as made of human and animal bones, heads, blood, and flesh, and the fires burning the sacrificial victims serving as lamps around her dwelling:

This temple of Kālī was enclosed by an enclosure wall and an entrance *gopura*, constructed with bones. This *gopura* was preceded by a *makaratorana* of iron erected by goblins. On the top of the enclosure walls, the severed heads of peacocks, the heads of men offered as sacrifice, the heads of young babies also severed in sacrifice and blood-oozing flesh as standards, were placed as beautifying elements. The *makaratorana* captured from the Pandyan capital, and the severed ears of war elephants were planted as swings. (Nagaswamy 25–27)

Here we can see an analogy with the fragmentation of Baba Yaga's house, constructed from bones and body parts, and the fence with skulls with radiating eyeballs that serve as lamps, as discussed in chapter 1. Such reduction to essence and the death imagery indicate that they both have magical powers and are mistresses of transformation, standing on the threshold of change between life and death.

The Goddess Dhūmāvatī

A less-known Mahāvidyā, Dhūmāvatī ("Smoke"), the crone goddess, has a special link to Baba Yaga.[3] She is represented as an old widow—the most inauspicious and undesirable state in Hindu society—with a wrinkled face, a long nose, broken teeth, dried, long breasts, and disheveled hair. She is dressed in rags, wears a garland of severed heads, and carries a skull-cup (Kinsley, *Tantric* 180; Frawley 126). She is portrayed seated in a motionless chariot accompanied by crows, seated on a crow, or sometimes pulled by carrion-eating birds. In texts such as the *Prapañcasārasāra-saṁgraha*, she is said to resemble a crow. She carries a broom, a winnowing basket, crushes bones in her mouth, and, like Kālī, dwells in unhospitable, uncivilized, and dangerous places. She is hungry, thirsty, quarrelsome, and rude. The crow is a symbol of bad luck, famine, and death (Leslie, "Śrī and Jyeṣṭā 119). Dhūmāvatī represents the opposite of what is considered pleasant and gentle, embodying the most undesirable traits, such as ugliness, lack, old age, and rejection—the aspects of reality that humans are afraid of and which they must confront through her. Nevertheless, Dhūmāvatī is said to transform herself, appearing in many forms—as a young maiden in the morning, a married woman at noon, or as a widow in the evening (Kinsley, *Tantric* 176, 180–91)—and revealing constant transformation. These characteristics make her a close cousin to the "outsider" and mistress of death and transformation, Baba Yaga.

Kālī and Other Fierce Divinities

What the divinities discussed in this book—Baba Yaga, Pombagira, and Santa Muerte—have in common becomes clearer when we examine the Hindu goddess Kālī, as well as the Yoruban Ìyàmi Òṣòròngà, the Sumerian Inanna, and the female deity from the Gnostic text "The Thunder, Perfect Mind." The primordial, all-encompassing goddesses of all creation, such as Inanna, Isis, and Ìyàmi Òṣòròngà, represent the Great Mother—the cosmos, the origin of all that is, the ultimate reality. Similarly, Kālī is "the sole Creatrix, Preserver, and Destructress of infinite millions of Worlds, has on Her Body the mark of the Yoni signifying creation, full breasts denoting preservation, and a terrible visage signifying the withdrawal of all things" (*Karpūrādi-stotra*, "Prayer" 45). Kālī's paradoxical nature, as one of the African ancestral mother of humanity, Ìyàmi Òṣòròngà, and of the feminine deity from the Gnostic text, "The Thunder, Perfect Mind," discussed in chapter 3, is powerful and all-encompassing. Her black color represents vitality, perfection, the cosmos, and the source of origins, as well as decomposition and death.

These concepts find a concrete representation in India in the bizarre figure of Kālī whose aspect and behavior are a challenge to, and the negation of, orderly and controlled society. Throughout the *Hymn to Kālī* (*Karpūrādi-stotra*), and the preceding "Prayer at the Feet of Śri Sri Kālīka" (44–48), Kālī is portrayed as black or dark blue, naked, with disheveled hair and a bloody mouth, wearing a garland of heads and a belt of severed hands, earrings of children's bones, a cup made of a human skull in one hand and a sword in the other; she sits on a corpse in the cremation ground, surrounded by bones, skulls, and female jackals. Her behavior is tempestuous, she slays demons in battle, gets drunk on blood and alcohol, laughs and howls wildly; she is frightening and awesome (figure 2.1). At other times, she is portrayed standing on a passive corpse of her husband, Śiva, engaged in reverse intercourse. Kālī, described as springing from goddess Durgā's forehead, is terrific and fearsome in her anger, as she severs the bonds of illusion. As Durgā, she slays and swallows demons, the *asuras*, devouring all existence:

> Bearing the strange skull-topped staff, decorated with a garland of skulls, clad in a tiger's skin, very appalling owing to her emaciated flesh, with gaping mouth, fearful with her tongue lolling out, having deep-sunk reddish eyes and filling the regions of the sky with her roars, and falling upon impetuously and slaughtering the great asuras in that army, she devoured those hosts of the foes of the devas. (*Devī-māhātmyam*C h.7:7–9)

Nevertheless, since Kālī embodies liberation and empowerment and, similar to her predecessor Koṯṯavai, was worshipped

Figure 2.1 Kālī by Maya Sokovic. Reproduced with permission of the artist

by a wide population in South Asia, it is not surprising that she came under the control of the Brahmanized elites and the British colonial rule. The goddess was "reconfigured as danger, chaos, and pollution"; was appropriated, tamed, domesticated, and sweetened; and her maternal aspects were emphasized. In addition, female shamans and oracles were converted into male religious specialists dressed in goddess attire (Caldwell, "Margins" 254–62). This process led to the transformation of Kālī in Bengal "from a wild, ferocious deity of death to a benign youthful mother." Moreover, during Kālī Pūjā, the most important Bengali Kālī festival, in the Kālīghat Temple in Calcutta, she is worshipped as the auspicious goddess Lakṣmī and no animal sacrifice takes place on that day. Kālī's terrific image is completely covered by a sari, jewelry, and garlands, showing only the face without blood or fangs, the hands, and part of the feet. Nevertheless, devotees still see her as both fierce and compassionate, sacrifice goats to her, and even offer her their ownblood. [4]

In spite of the attempts to tame her, Kālī's ferocious and independent aspects still persist, even when she is reconfigured as mother. As Baba Yaga, Pombagira, and Santa Muerte are dual, ambiguous, and paradoxical, so is the Hindu goddess Kālī who is described by the eighteenth-century Bengali poet-saint Rāmprasād in the following way:

> Mother,inc omparablya rrayed,
> Hair flying, stripped down,
> You battle-dance on Shiva's heart,
> A garland of heads that bounce off
> Your heavy hips, chopped-off hands
> For a belt, the bones of infants
> For earrings, and the lips,
> The teeth like jasmine, the face
> A lotus blossomed, the laugh,
> And the dark body boiling up and out
> Like a storm cloud, and those feet
> Whose beauty is only deepened by blood.
> So Prasad cries: My mind is dancing! (Sen 65)

Kālī's outfit is reminiscent of Baba Yaga's hut, which represents Yaga herself. As described earlier, the hut is made of human body parts, is surrounded with a fence of human bones topped with skulls, and has a jaw with sharp teeth for a lock. In addition, Baba Yaga has a "bony leg" and she spins a thread made of bones and entrails of the dead, connecting the spiritual and material realms, similar to the African Àjẹ́/Àwọn Iyá Wa ("Our Mothers"). The Aztec goddess Coatlicue is adorned with skulls and snakes (see figure I.1). Kālī, especially in her form of Guhyakālī, similar to Baba Yaga and Coatlicue, is also associated with snakes that are linked to the underworld—the realm of the dead—as well as to transformation, renewal, and immortality. For example, in the Indian Muṭiyēṯṯu ritual performance, Bhadrakālī's headdress is covered with serpent hoods and snakes encircle the breasts of the actor's costume. Fangs and the movement of the tongue are also reminiscent of snakes (Caldwell, *Terrifying* 144). According to some Medieval Tamil texts, Kālī's temple was not only made of severed heads, bones, flesh, and blood, but gold and precious gems were imbedded in the structures (Nagaswamy 25), treasures reminiscent of the ones kept by Baba Yaga.

Like other powerful deities discussed in this book, Kālī is portrayed as independent and childless in the literal sense, but simultaneously she is the great "Mother of the Universe":

> O Mother, Thou givest birth to and protectest the world, and at the time of dissolution dost withdraw to Thyself the earth and all things; therefore Thou art Brahmā, and the Lord of the three worlds, the Spouse of Śri, and Maheśa, and all other beings and things. Ah Me! How, then, shall I praise Thy greatness? (*Karpūrādi-stotra* 12:78)

The new emphasis on her sweetened motherliness can be seen in Rāmprasād's devotional poem, as the mother of her vulnerable children that adore her:

> I shall take refuge in my Mother's feet; where shall I go at this time of my distress?
>
> (Sinha12:6)

Nevertheless, she is not a consistent mother:

> I am not calling you Mother anymore,
> All you give me is trouble. (Sen 35)

The formidable pan-African Ìyàmi Òṣòròngà, ancestress of Pombagira, is also described as the "All-powerful mother.../ who climbs high and looks down on earth" (Beier 10–11); Baba Yaga's functions, as she transmutes matter and is the mistress of life and death, are reminiscent of Kālī and the Great Mother; and Santa Muerte is often addressed by her devotees as the all-powerful and protecting "Mother" who can solve all problems and who has the power to give and take away.

In addition, both Kālī and Pombagira are linked to divine possession trances, advice giving, sexuality, rage, violent behavior, blood sacrifice, alcohol, and the colors red and black, universal aspects that have been removed from the Virgin Mary persona. Moreover, they are both polyvalent, having many "paths" or avatars (e.g., Tārā and Durgā for Kālī and Maria Padilha and Maria Mulambo for Pombagira). They also play important roles in their women devotees' liberation and empowerment. As Pombagira is accompanied by her sacred songs—*pontos cantados*—and diagrams—*pontos riscados*—Kālī has her sacred songs and diagrams or *yantras* that symbolize the whole universe in miniature (Caldwell, *Terrifying* 1). These designs that focus on creative sexual energy, with elements such as the triangle or two superimposed triangles, with a dot in the middle, the lotus, and the circle, which symbolize the vulva, sexual union, the male seed, and the womb (Frawley 242; Kṛṣṇanānda Āgamavāgiśa 929–82), have to be drawn before the possession ceremony or performance takes place.

Possession Trances

An important part of the devotion to Devī ("Goddess"), especially in northern India, are the sacred trances experienced by female devotees that are reportedly one of the few places for empowerment of women. As in the case of Brazil Umbanda's Pombagira, a woman can be "chosen" by an entity (*entidade*) to serve her through embodiment in divine possession trances,[5] during which she speaks with the deity's voice and gives advice to devotees. The problems that can be remedied by advice, rituals, and offerings prescribed by the embodied goddess range from physical, mental, or undefined illness to family and marital disturbances, employment and legal troubles, including harm provoked by malefic forces, as well as study-related. Similar troubles are addressed by the Mexican unofficial saint Santa Muerte, discussed in chapter 4. Through their sacred roles as the goddess mediums, women in India and in Brazil may attain financial independence, respect, and status that are otherwise unattainable to them in poor, male-oriented societies. Not only can they transgress traditional gender roles and avoid marriage, but they can also give strength and empowerment to others.[6] As the Indian goddesses, including Kālī, embody *śakti*—the divine, feminine creative power and energy of the universe—the Brazilian *orixás* ("gods" and "goddesses") and entities, such as Pombagira, embody the spiritual energy, *axé*, that pervades and animates all things and therefore can be used to perform cures and achieve diverse goals.

Diasporic Kālī

The consideration of practices connected to the diasporic devotion to Kālī in Trinidad, manifested in local Kali Pujas, brings Kālī even closer to Pombagira. These weekly ceremonies include spirit possession and advice giving by mediums, blood sacrifice, liquor, drum playing, and "wild" dancing, among other practices. In addition, a syncretic accommodation is clearly visible during the feast for Siparee Mai ("Mother of Siparia") in southern Trinidad, where Mother Kālī is identified with the Catholic Virgin Mary or La Divina Pastora ("Holy Shepherdess"). A similar co-optation by the Catholic Church of the dark patroness of the Roma, Sara-La-Kâli, takes place at Les Saintes Maries-de-la-Mer in southern France. Although she is not an officially accepted Catholic saint, her most revered representation stands in the subterranean crypt of the local Catholic Church, surrounded by thousands of lit candles. In addition, a holy mass, a church procession, and a subsequent submersion of her statue into the sea take place every year on May 24 (figure 2.2). This procession is similar to the Durgā Pūjā, a yearly ceremony performed to the goddess Durgā, Kālī's avatar, in Calcutta.[7] I also

Figure 2.2 Procession for Sara-La-Kâli, Les Saintes Maries-de-la-Mer, France, 2008. Photo by author

observed a pilgrimage to the ocean of a Virgin Mary–like statue of the Brazilian version of this figure, Kali Sara or Sara Kali, in Rio de Janeiro in 2009. In Brazil, she is still very marginal and has not been incorporated by the Catholic Church, which has to deal with a myriad of African-derived syncretic religions. In fact, Kali Sara is usually worshipped in the same temples as Umbanda entities, but she is linked to the Catholic patroness of Brazil, the black Our Lady Aparecida (see figure 3.2), and can be seen as a counterpart to the demonized Pombagira.

In addition, Kālī has been incorporated and accommodated into the multilayered worship practices of Kali Mai Puja in the polysemic context of Guyana, where African, East Indian, and subjacent Aboriginal spiritual traditions merge.[8] Here, as in other Latin American locations discussed in this book, the population that participates in the worship of Kali Mai Puja has been stricken by poverty and political impotence and therefore is desperate for supernatural help. Kālī, being the "outsider" and simultaneously the universal mother, is believed to be very powerful, and thus the ideal protector of the dispossessed and the powerless. Moreover, through her several hands she embodies the ability to make things happen and execute change, so needed by her worshippers. Like them, she is dark in appearance, and like the sacred coconut, she embodies light born of obscurity—she is dark on the outside and bright with the transcendent light of truth and knowledge on the inside.[9] In another syncretic development, the Black Madonna of Einsiedeln, Switzerland, is worshipped by Hindu Tamil refugees as their goddess or as a "Christian Kālī."[10]

It is interesting to note how the fierce Indian goddess Kālī has been reappropriated and tamed in the context of the Romani diaspora in France and Brazil, as well as in the Indian diaspora in Trinidad, Guyana, and Switzerland. Kālī's versatility and adaptability in the aforementioned locations mimic the flexibility and ability of renewal of her worshippers, as well as of other divine female figures analyzed in this book, that play a protective role in marginalized populations. In the next two chapters, I will be looking at liminal, outsider divinities in the context of Latin American societies of the twentieth and twenty-first centuries.

PART II

Latin America

CHAPTER 3

Pombagira, the Holy Streetwalker

With my red dress
I come to the ceremony
With my necklace, earring and bracelet,
I come to work!
I use the best perfumes,
To please everybody,
I am Pomba-Gira,
Andle t'sw ork![1]

[The] sorceresses were seen lying on their backs in the fields or woods, naked above the navel and gesticulating with their forearms and thighs. They keep their limbs in an arrangement suitable for that filthy act, while the incubus demons work with them invisibly.

—MacKay313

While Baba Yaga and Kālī are ancient Eurasian threshold divinities, mainly expressed by symbols of death and decomposition, transformation, the womb, ambiguity, and wilderness, Pombagira and Santa Muerte are contemporary examples of liminal personae that appeared as a consequence of crisis, "a weakening and eventual suspension of the ordinary, taken-for-granted structures of life" (Szakolczai 156), in the changing socioeconomic conditions of twentieth-century Latin America. They are polyvalent and mobile, and they excel in liminal activities while dwelling in peripheral areas of society and the world. Their worshippers are equally marginalized in their respective milieus in Brazil and Mexico, often being outsiders and holding an inferior status.

The Brazilian entity Pombagira may be considered a twentieth-century avatar of the ancient, fierce life and death goddess Queen of the Universe and her priestess representative on earth—the sacred virgin/prostitute—that was later demonized.[2] Like the syncretic Umbanda religion she is part of, Pombagira is a new creation with roots going back to Europe and Africa. This chapter, based on my fieldwork in Brazil as well as on ample literature, looks at her origin, history, characteristics, and devotion, while examining the reasons for and the implications of this veneration for the lives of her devotees, as well as her place in the Brazilian religious and social landscape.

Background

In 1996, I was living in Brazil while conducting fieldwork on the Candomblé religion and its *orixás* ("gods" and "goddesses"),[3] omnipresent in the ancient Portuguese viceroyalty's capital Salvador da Bahia. It has been said that Brazil is the country that has more Afro-descendants than any other place in the world, outside of Nigeria,[4] with a special concentration in the northeastern state of Bahia. I was fascinated with the religion, the orixás, and their all-encompassing presence and appeal in Brazilian society and beyond. African religious practices[5] that had been suppressed for several centuries erupted to the surface with full strength in the 1980s, after they became legal. As a consequence, during several months of my stay in Salvador, I hardly met anyone who would not be overtly involved in them in some way, from the inhabitants of the popular neighborhoods and shantytowns at the outskirts of Salvador to those of elegant areas where renowned intellectuals and politicians from Brazil and abroad resided. What I initially wasn't aware of was that there were still other layers of syncretic religiosity, not as chic to belong to, but which were even more widespread than Candomblé. Among them was Umbanda, a newer, twentieth-century urban religion that combined several practices, including African, Native Brazilian, Catholic, and Spiritist. On the other hand, Candomblé has been "re-Africanized" by means of a conscious effort to revive the African tradition, which included study, travels to Nigeria, and stripping of a Catholic veneer, imposed during colonial times. My first glance at the Umbanda entity Pombagira took place when a professional Brazilian woman friend of mine showed me, at her house in Salvador's historical Santo Antônio neighborhood, a statuette of a half-naked woman with flowing hair, to whom she offered liquor and cigarettes because she was "the protector of women" (figure 3.1).

This image aroused my interest and curiosity. It made me wonder what other women-empowering elements, beside Candomblé's matriarchal organization, were hidden in Afro-Brazilian religions. My dealings with this entity were for years limited to discussions at conferences, often in regard to

Figure 3.1 Pombagira house altar, Salvador, Bahia, Brazil, 1996. Photo by author

Argentina, and unexpected encounters during a stay in Uruguay in 2006. It wasn't until a trip to Rio de Janeiro in 2009, in search of Santa Sara Kali—a "Gypsy Black Madonna,"[6] that I rediscovered Pombagira. She appeared as the street woman and female devil, together with the *malandro* ("scroundel") Zé Pilintra, as part of the powerful *povo da rua* or "street people" of U mbanda/Quimbanda.[7]

Origin and Name

Pombagira is a female trickster figure. The archaic trickster persona is present in myths and folktales around the world. He/she is always an outsider and a marginal character that cannot be trusted, characterized by an excessive behavior. An example is the Greek god Hermes—associated with ambivalence and liminal activities like language, commerce, transport, and sexuality. Other examples are Loki in Skandinavia, the Flemish Reynard the fox, the Italian Pulcinella and Arlechino, the Native American coyote, and the Yoruba Eshu (Exu) (Szakolczai 152, 154). Pombagira, in her different avatars, is a Brazilian female version of Exu and as such is famous for being insatiable, promiscuous, vulgar, and talkative.

The multifarious Pombagira is one of the most powerful entities of Umbanda, a religion discussed further in this chapter. Her name and persona appear to be a synthesis and a reinterpretation of several popular traditions. According to Monique Augras, Pombagira was "born" as a transformation of Bombonjira, a Congo name for the Yoruba god Exu, mediator, trickster, and a phallic deity, into Bombagira and then Pombagira. An analysis of this name is revealing, as *gira* is the name of an Umbanda ritual and means "action of circling" in Portuguese, as well as "path" (*nila/njira*) in Bantu. In Portuguese, *pomba* means "pigeon" and is slang for the masculine sexual organs in the northeast and the feminine sexual organs in the south of Brazil. On the other hand, for the BaKongo, *pemba* is the white clay that cleanses and signifies "the mountain of the dead"; in Yorubaland, it symbolizes

Obatalá,[8] the orisa *funfun* ("white") (Washington 67). Pombagira may also be associated with the Àwọn Ìyá Wa (*iyá mi*), the powerful, awe-inspiring, and independent African ancestral mothers, manifested in today's Afro-Brazilian worship of female orixás such as the *iabás* Nanã, Obá, Iemanjá, Oxum, Ewa, and Iansã/Oyá (Santos, Os nàgô e a morte 114–17). According to informants, for the iabás that carry a sword, such as the queen of the oceans Iemanjá, a castrated male animal is sacrificed (Augras "De Iyá mi" 23, 25, 32). From these orixás, Iansã (Oyá) and Nanã have a more immediate connection with Pombagira. This is expressed by the following Pombagira's *ponto cantado*[9]:

> Inhansāw hoga vey ous trength
> Is Queenof C andomblé
> Let's go praise the Queen
> Pomba Gira She-Devil Woman.[10]

CHARACTERISTICS

As her African and European predecessors, Pombagira is a powerful persona. She is addressed formally as *dona, senhora*, or *você* and by her name.[11] It has been revealed that a close relationship with her can be the source of strength, protection, autonomy, recognition, and prestige for women who keep an altar to her at their homes. Moreover, a Pombagira, prototype of a prostitute, embodies transgressive femininity, is sexually independent, unsubduable, and the antithesis of a docile and maternal housewife. According to one ponto cantado: "She is the wife of seven husbands,/Do not provoke her,/Pombagira is dangerous."[12] Therefore, thanks to her, mediums may be able to reinterpret their traditional domestic roles and stand up to their abusive husbands (Hayes, "Fogos cruzados" 86–92). This is illustrated by another ponto cantado: "Pombagira is a tamer/Of fierce donkeys/I have tamed my husband/With six hundred thousand devils."[13] This song echoes the following one, which has kept its Iberian character: "My little San Anthony/Taimer of a brave bull/Whoever provokes Maria Padilha/Is provoking the devil." In Bahia, Santo Antônio corresponds to the orixá Ogum, to whom the Exus are subordinated.[14] Pombagira only incorporates in women, homosexuals, and transgender individuals—usually the inferior and marginalized elements of society. Her subaltern and liminal position allows transgressions that bestow strength, power, and independence on Pombagira, whose sexuality is divorced from a reproductive role and who is always linked to the idea of prostitution. As an embodiment of the rejected "other," she is not subject to societal rules and can freely exercise her sexual power. The following Pombagira song reflects her condition:

> Pomba-Gira is her destiny
> My destiny is this:
> Is to have fun!
> I drink, I smoke, I jump and dance,
> In order to subsist!
> Thus I carry out my destiny,
> Which is only to have fun![15]

This unrestrained relationship with sexuality and the street, typical of liminal personae, is perceived as dangerous by structured, male-dominated South American society, where the woman's place has traditionally been that of a virginal mother at home. An analogy can be found in India, where fierce, uncontrollable goddesses, such as Kālī, which represent destruction and regeneration of life as well as sexuality, are also connected to blood sacrifice, alcohol, and spirit possession.[16] Moreover, according to Erndl, possession rituals in northern Indian villages are one of the very few spaces of empowerment for women ("Play" 156–57).

Pombagira, the Exu-Mulher ("She-Devil Woman"), is a fascinating and ambiguous entity; like Baba Yaga, Santa Muerte, and Kālī, she is dangerous, even considered by some a female devil, but at the same time she is trusted and invoked for strength, protection, and support, as she is in possession of magical powers, similar to the powerful pan-African Àwọn Ìyá

Wa ("Our Mothers") or Àwọn Ìyàmi Òṣòròngà ("The Great and Mysterious Mother"), discussed further in this chapter. She is a prototype of a harlot, a woman who rebels against the traditional female role, as confirmed by her "seven husbands." Pombagira is associated with dangerous transition places of exchange, such as the crossroads, thresholds, cemeteries, markets, beaches, and garbage deposits (in the case of Maria Molambo—"Raggedy Pombagira," and Pombagira da Lixeira—"Garbage Pombagira"). A related goddess in ancient Mexico was Tlazolteotl, the "Eater of Filth," goddess of creation of life associated with the earth, fertility, childbirth, sexuality, venereal disease, as well as of healing and forgiveness. Her dual nature brought both suffering and its cure and was connected to sexual deviance and ritual girl prostitution. In the Aztec *codices* ("codexes"), she was portrayed squatting while giving birth and sometimes defecating. It is also interesting to note that as Pombagiras are connected to possession trances, advice giving, alcohol, blood sacrifice, cemeteries and garbage deposits, and the colors red and black, shamanistic and Tantric rituals for the goddess Kālī in India also involve possession and advice by the shaman, blood sacrifice, as well as drinking alcohol in such spiritually polluted places as cremation grounds. Kālī's preferred colors are also red and black.[17] In India, as in Mexico and Brazil, sacrificial blood is considered the life energy of the universe. While in the interpretation of Gypsy spirits in Brazil the female energy is separated into two extremes—Sara Kali and Pombagira[18]—in India, this energy or *śakti* may be personified as powerful and ferocious divinities, in benign forms, or in the case of the dual mother goddess Kālī, who unites opposite poles in one entity, as both creator and destroyer, terrifying and beneficent.[19]

Types of Pombagiras

There are different types of "families" of Pombagiras in Brazil: Pombagiras Ciganas ("Gypsy Pombagiras"), Marias Molambo

("Raggedy Pombagiras"), Pombagiras "cruzadas" da Linha das Almas ("crossed" Pombagiras of the Line of the Souls), and Pombagiras Meninas or "Virgin Child Pombagiras," among others. Some of the most widely known of them are Pombagira Rainha das Sete Encruzulhadas ("Queen of the Seven Crossroads"), Rainha do Cruzeiro ("Queen of the Cross"), da Encruzilhada ("of the Crossroads"), da Figueira ("of the Fig Tree"), da Calunga ("of the Cemetery"), das Sete Calungas ("of the Seven Cemeteries"), da Porteira ("of the Gate"), da Sepultura ("of the Sepulcre"), das Sete Sepulturas ("of the Seven Sepulcres"), das Sete Sepulturas Rasas ("of the Seven Shallow Sepulcres"), Cigana ("Gypsy"), do Cemitério ("of the Cemetery"), da Praia ("of the Beach"), das Almas ("of the Souls"), Maria Padilha, Pombagira Quitéria, Pombagira Sete Saias ("Seven Skirts"), Pombagira Dama da Noite ("Lady of the Night"), and Pombagira Mirongueira ("Sorceress"), among others (Molina 9–10; Prandi, "Pombagiras" 95). The names indicate their wide scope from the poorest to the wealthiest and from the innocent to the most experienced and "impure," echoing the all-encompassing nature of the African Àwọn Ìyá Wa. Their dwelling places and times are liminal par excellence—connected to death, cemeteries, and the night. As in the case of Santa Muerte, discussed in chapter 4, Pombagiras are considered very mighty and magical, and they receive requests for healing, for help in financial and love affairs, and for attacks against someone. Their specialty is the realm of love and sexuality, and they are known to respond to any request without limitations, "[a]s if there existed a world of happiness, access to which is controlled and governed by her, that would be the exact opposite of our frustrating everyday world" (Prandi, "Pombagiras" 101).

A particular case among Pombagiras is the most refined of them, Maria Padilha. This persona is based on the historical noblewoman María Padilla, lover of Don Pedro I of Castile (1334–1368), between 1352 and 1361, by whom she had four children. Because of María, at 18 years old he left his wife, Blanca de Borbón. María Padilla was immortalized in this role in the sixteenth-century Castilian *Romancero general*. She was later included by Prosper Mérimée in his novella *Carmen* (1845) and adapted into the homonymous opera by Georges Bizet, first performed in 1875. Mérimée presented María Padilla/Carmen as Bari Crillisa, the queen of the Gypsies. Nevertheless, this certainly is a mythification of this figure, as the Roma did not arrive in Western Europe until the fifteenth century, and at that time the "others" of the Iberian Peninsula included mainly Jews and Moors, who were the ones usually accused of witchcraft. In fact, the wizard of the *Romancero* is a Jew (Augras, "María Padilla" 304–308). In 1841, Gaetano Donizetti's opera *Maria Padilla* was performed in Milan, Italy, and in 1856 in Rio de Janeiro, Brazil. Maria Padilla was diabolized in the process (Capone, *A busca* 110–14) and became one of the avatars of Pombagira in Brazil. When we examine one of Maria Padilha's *pontos cantados*,

> Where does Maria Padilha come from?
> Where does Maria Padilha live?
> She lives in the gold mine
> Where the black cock sings
> Where the child does not cry,[20]

we notice a similarity with ancient European magical incantations. The gold mine that symbolizes the riches in the womb of the earth reminds us of Ayé ("The Earth")—one of the names of the African Great Mothers—as well as of the temples of Old Europe from before 4,000 BC,[21] and of Baba Yaga who guards her gold, silver, and copper treasures.[22] The black cock is connected to death, the underworld, fertility, and the Black Goddess of death and rebirth (Kopliński 151; Walker, *Dictionary* 397; Kohli 190). Another attribute of Maria Padilha is the ficus tree, the dwelling place of the spirits of the dead in Afro-Brazilian religions.

Devotional Centers and the Public Sphere

Pombagira Cigana and Maria Padilha are related to the *Linea de Oriente* or Ciganos ("Gypsy") entities of Umbanda, from which also the unofficial saintly figure of Sara Kali evolved. Nevertheless, in the worship centers where she is included, Sara Kali is kept separate from the entities of Umbanda and is placed on altars together with such Catholic holy figures as Jesus Christ and Nossa Senhora Aparecida ("Our Lady Aparecida") (figure 3.2). This is the case at the Tzara Ramirez religious center where I conducted fieldwork in 2009. At this center, located in the peripheral Rio de Janeiro neighborhood Nova Iguaçú, the practices are syncretic, with a strong connection to Kardecist Spiritism[23] and New Age practices. The Cigano ("Gypsy") entities practice "charity" by giving counsel to individuals, and the overall belief in reincarnation and Karmic

Figure 3.2 Altar with Sara Kali, Jesus Christ, and Nossa Senhora Aparecida, Tzara Ramirez, Rio de Janeiro, Brazil, 2009. Photo by author

evolution is apparent (figure 3.3). Many rooms are devoted to Eastern and New Age healing practices, such as pranic rituals, shiatsu massage, work with crystals, and chromotherapy, and are adorned with images of Hindu gods and goddesses. Syncretism is also obvious through strong connections to Catholicism and Candomblé, manifested in prayers such as Our Father, Ave Maria, and chants to Oxalá, an orixá syncretized with Jesus Christ. In addition, Marcelo (João Marcelo Vidal, alias Anrez Ramirez), the *barô* or leader of Tzara Ramirez, is also a *babalorixá* ("priest") of a nearby Candomblé *terreiro* of 120 initiates (figure 3.4).[24] Similarly, in the case of Santa Muerte, discussed in chapter 4, there are strong influences from Catholicism and Afro-Cuban Santaría. My visit to Marcelo's *roça*[25] revealed its close connection to Umbanda through the inclusion of such entities as Exus and Pombagiras and their symbols (figures 3.5–3.7). This highly syncretic practice approximates

Figure 3.3 Gypsy entities incarnated into mediums practice "charity," Tzara Ramirez, Rio de Janeiro, Brazil, 2009. Photo by author

Figure 3.4 Barô Marcelo in front of his Candomblé *terreiro*, Rio de Janeiro, Brazil, 2009. Photo by author

the Omolocô religion (see table 3.1). On the other hand, at the Templo dos Ciganos Encantados in the marginal Rio de Janeiro neighborhood Quintino, the worship of Santa Sara Kali is clearly connected to Umbanda/Quimbanda. Here, Santa Sara is accompanied by two Caboclas ("female Indian ancestor spirits")—Iara and Jurema—as well as by the popular Ciganos figures—Carmencita and Vladimir—and the Catholic Our Lady Aparecida. There are also statues of different Umbandist/Quimbandist entities, such as Prêtos Velhos, Caboclos, as well as Pombagiras and Exus. Although they have a very significant presence at this religious center, I was strictly forbidden to photograph the latter "spirits of the left."

Pombagira is a persona present in many areas of Brazilian life, from literature and song, to soap operas, journalism, and

Figure 3.5 Exu Zé Pilintra at Marcelo's *terreiro*, Rio de Janeiro, Brazil, 2009. Photo by author

police investigations (Prandi, "Pombagiras" 98). A particular example is a judiciary case in Rio de Janeiro in 1979–1981 that was brought to the public sphere by press articles, in which Pombagira was accused of inciting a woman to commit a crime against an abusive and impotent husband. In this homicide case, the person incorporating Pombagira Maria Padilha, as well as the wife of the victim, and two other accomplices were judged in court and sentenced to 14–20 years in prison each. Among the experts called to help and solve the case were an Umbanda *pai-de-santo* ("priest"), a Pentecostal minister, and a psychiatrist.[26] Similarly, Kelly Hayes in her book *Holy Harlots* brings up an "unresolved" murder case in which the reader can infer that the victim was eliminated by the medium possessed by Pombagira because *aquela moça* ("that gal") was the medium husband's slov er.

Figure 3.6 Pombagira Cigana at Marcelo's *terreiro*, Rio de Janeiro, Brazil, 2009. Photo by author

Figure 3.7 Symbols of Exu at Marcelo's *terreiro*, Rio de Janeiro, Brazil, 2009. Photo by author.

Gypsy Entities

An unofficial saint figure that contrasts with Pombagira is Santa Sara Kali, discussed earlier, who evolved as a separate entity from the *Linea de Oriente* or Ciganos ("Gypsies") of Umbanda about 10–20 years ago, as a consequence of a very successful telenovela ("soap opera"). *Explode coração* was featured on TV Globo in the 1990s, and as a result a revival in the interest in the Roma culture took place. The Roma have been romanticized in the process.[27] A curious "coincidence" is that Pombagira of the Umbanda religion always wears red and black, traditionally worn by real-life Gypsies, but usually forbidden at the *tzaras* devoted to the worship of Santa Sara Kali and other "Gypsy" and New Age-related deities and practices. One of the pontos cantados that identify Pombagira when she appears embodied in a medium during an Umbanda ceremony is: "Dressed in red and black/In the night she brings a mystery/She is a beautiful young woman/Whirling, whirling, whirling there."[28] The colors red and black are related to Exus and Pombagiras. According to Washington, in African belief systems, red is related to blood and the power to make things happen, white to spiritual transcendence, and black to origins, perfection, and vitality. Turner suggests that these colors correspond to red, white, and black bodily fluids and, as the human body may be seen as a microcosm of the universe, they constitute the totality of the cosmos.[29]

As reality requires a balance of opposites and one extreme cannot exist without the other, it is not surprising that while searching for Saint Sara Kali, the virginal Romani Madonna, I also found her complementary side—Pombagira—housed in the same quarters. One of her avatars is in fact called Pombagira Cigana or "Gypsy Pombagira" and another one—Maria Padilha—a legendary-historical figure with alleged Spanish Gypsy ascendance. Nevertheless, I believe that these figures have little to do with "real" Gypsies themselves and more with superimposed layers of ancient female divinities from different cultures, as well as with daily life circumstances of urban Brazil. There is also a necessity to countervail the official "good" Virgin Mary and docile orixás, such as Oxum, with their fierce counterparts. Other orixás, such as Iemanjá—queen of the oceans—always included tempestuous aspects, but because of her syncretism with the Virgin Mary, and her widespread presence in Brazilian society, her public images have been dulcified (figure 3.8). In fact, the only orixás that today have any direct kinship with Pombagira are Iansã (Oyá)—an independent fiery woman, counterpart of the orixá Xangô, connected to wind, fire, spirits, and cemeteries—and Nanã, an old female orixá, related to the Àwọn Ìyá Wa.

Figure 3.8 Dulcified image of goddess Iemanjá, Salvador, Bahia, Brazil, 1996. Photo by author

Umbanda, Exus, and Marginality

To understand the Pombagira entity, we need to consider the context in which she appears, that of Umbanda, a modern religion from urban Brazil. It is believed that Umbanda, with its "inferior" and liminal entities, such as Pombagiras, appeared as a consequence of rapid industrialization and massive migration of marginalized individuals from rural areas as well as from abroad to large cities such as Rio de Janeiro and Sao Paulo, at the turn of the nineteenth century.[30] Umbanda does not deal with death or with salvation of the soul, but, rather, is a religion of life, concerned with the manipulation of daily reality. It is a practice geared toward everyday survival in difficult life circumstances, used to alleviate afflictions of the body, the mind, and the spirit. Ill health, love, and financial problems, as well as other areas of daily subsistence that require constant attention, are a special focus of Umbanda. These disorders of reality require a mystic cure, which

> is only comprehensible in relation to the official one. The patients who go to the consultation of Umbanda are those whose sufferings are not covered by the classificatory device of the medical agency; who have not obtained a diagnosis or whose diagnosis has not led to a cure. The Umbandist classificatory tools operate thus in the interstice of the official, on their margin, and, at the same time, against them. (Brumana and Martinez 218, 254–55)

The liminality of Umbanda entities such as Exus and Pombagiras bestows them with unusual power. They are inferior, rejected by the official structure, and their domain is also marginal—the street, the crossroads, the market, and the cemetery—places of transition, ambiguity, and insecurity, in which, nonetheless, they know how to operate. This is opposite to the privileged sectors of society, for most of which these places are off limits; they are only places of transition, not their dwelling places. But people in certain occupations, such as street vendors, prostitutes, taxi drivers, policemen, and thieves, also dwell in these places, and they often seek the aid and protection of special entities, such as Exus and Pombagiras in Brazil and Santa Muerte in Mexico.[31]

Pombagira is a Brazilian creation, a unique female form of Exu, who is the messenger and mediator African god with characteristics of a trickster. His colors are red and black, and his symbol is fire (figure 3.9). In Afro-Brazilian religions such as Candomblé, Exu is the dynamic, propelling principle, responsible for communication. This orixá of destiny and the crossroads, who opens the paths for any enterprise, is the first to be given reverence in any ceremony. During the Padê propitiatory ritual that precedes all public *festas* ("ceremonies") in the traditional, mainly Ketu Candomblés of Bahia, offerings are given to Exu, so he can transfer them to the feminine and the masculine ancestors, the iyá mi and the *baba egún*, and through them to all the elements of the universe. Thus, he is in charge of communicating and restituting the *axé* ("divine force" or "spiritual

Figure 3.9 Representation of Exu, Rio de Janeiro, Brazil, 2009. Photo by author

power") of the mythical ancestors and ensuring a harmonious relationship that allows the continuation of the vital cycle. During the most outstanding moment of this ritual, the mighty Àwọn Ìyàmi Òṣòròngà[32] is inv oked:

> Owner of magnificent wings, my mother Òṣòròngà.
> Owner of magnificent wings, my mother Òṣòròngà.
> I salute you, do not kill me, my mother.
> I salute you, do not cause me disturbances my mother.
> If you come close to us, oh protect us![33]

It is believed that, thanks to the performance of Candomlé's *padê* (ritual for Exu), calamities such as disease, death, disturbance, and malediction will be conquered and that harmony and abundance will be maintained (Santos 184, 194–95). On the other hand, in Umbanda, Exus are identified with spirits of particular persons from the past, and they are divided onto "superior" and "inferior" "non-baptized" Exus, such as Zé Pilintra[34] and the Pombagiras, which are seen as demonic forces. Exu spirits do the "dirty work" the orixás cannot perform, they are considered their "slaves," and they only obey "the logic of the marketplace" of a capitalist society (Hayes, *Holy* 193). It is also believed that every living being has its personal Exu.

In Umbanda, as in Candomblé, the majority of participants seek a terreiro or religious community for help with their physical or emotional ailments, for which they could not find a cure at a doctor's office because they could not afford such a luxury, or because the help needed was outside and beyond the area of possibilities of any officially accepted practices. Belonging to a terreiro, with its regular rituals, such as *giras* ("ceremonies"), consultation with guides, divination, *despachos* ("offerings"), and other *obrigações* ("obligations"), alleviates or eliminates the initiates' problems. In the practice of Umbanda/Quimbanda, we can also find *macumbas* or attempts to harm someone, which can be regarded as ways of remedying scarcity. The word "macumba" has several meanings, from Afro-Brazilian possession religions in general to an "offering," to sorcery or "works of the left" (*da esquerda*). According to Brumana and Martinez, Macumbas, *mirongas*, or "works," in the latter sense, are equivalent to attempts to obtain some gain by damaging someone else. In the case of the macumbas, "the question of scarcity is symbolically dramatized and solved: To give is to take from another" (231, 237–38). *Trabalhos* or "works" are thus magical practices geared toward helping afflicted individuals. In the Umbandist universe, a miraculous cure may be attained through symbolic manipulation in which Pombagira is often the mediator.

Umbanda, which similarly to Pentecostalism has been called "a cult of affliction"[35] able to empower the powerless, is a highly syncretized Brazilian religion that started in Rio de Janeiro at the beginning of the twentieth century. According to several writers, its beginnings are associated with abrupt cultural and structural changes related to industrialization and migration (Fry, "Duas respostas" 75–76), which created a need for more effective, magical help on every level of subsistence. It has been said that Umbanda incorporates the four races and traditions that form the Brazilian society—African, European, Native Brazilian, and Oriental—and for this reason it is the "most Brazilian" or "authentically Brazilian" religion (Pereira 137). Nevertheless, it would be more precise to qualify those elements as African, Native Brazilian, Catholic, Spiritist, and Occultist, as this religion derives in part from Kardecist Spiritism.[36] Umbanda symbolically reverts the structure of power in Brazilian society, giving strength to the inferior entities "of the left," such as Exus and Pombagiras, and, by extension, to the marginalized individuals that practice the religion. By including representations of street folk, Indians, and slaves, it subverts the dominant discourse. Brumana and Martinez argue that Umbanda is a microcosm and the main expression of Brazilian culture, as well as "one of the few mediations which exist in Brazilian society between the radically excluded and the social spaces from which this exclusion is determined and effected, which has its roots in slavery" (294–95, 300).

This situation of marginalization and outsiderhood was further continued through the large migrations of the nineteenth and twentieth centuries to more industrialized regions of the country. The following ponto cantado stresses Pombagira's link to the power of Africa:

> I am Maria Padilha
> Of the 7 Crosses
> I have strength of the Souls
> Of the old ones from captivity
> We work together,
> In the same armful,
> I am Maria Padilha
> Well loved and beautiful.[37]

Umbanda terreiros or *tendas* ("religious centers") include worship of entities that enter into the bodies of their *burros* or *cavalos* ("donkeys" or "horses") during trances.[38] Then these mediums act as particular spirits from the past and give support and advice to people. They may assume behaviors of their spirits, strikingly different from the character of the persons that incorporate them. The comportment may be violent and lascivious, and it may involve vulgar speech and laughter or blood rituals.[39] Unlike in Candomblé, smoking and drinking are allowed in Umbanda, and the entities talk, giving advice to people through their mediums and thus practicing *caridade* ("charity"). Interestingly, *veshyas*, the East Indian sacred harlots, were also considered the embodiment of kindness or *charis*, the root word for "charity." Cigar smoke is known in Native American traditional cultures to induce states of trance and clairvoyance, and it is also included in Cuban Santería worship. This practice is in turn believed to allow spiritual growth and reincarnation in a more evolved form. The *oferendas* or "offerings" in Umbanda are preferably done outside the terreiro, in places such as the crossroads or the beach (figure 3.10), as their main entities dwell outdoors, while in Candomblé they are usually doneins ide.

Figure 3.10 Umbanda offering at the beach, Angra dos Reis, Brazil, 2009. Photo by author

In African and Afro-Brazilian philosophical thought, there is a strong belief in the continuity between god and the orixás, the spirits of the dead, and human beings. The eclectic Umbandist pantheon comprises different figures, such as God and the orixás or *santidades* ("holy figures"); and *entidades* ("entities") that include Caboclos ("Indians"), Prêtos Velhos ("old slaves"), Oguns ("soldiers"), Bahianos ("people from the Brazilian northeast"), Marujos or Marinheiros ("sailors"), Boiadeiros ("cowboys"), Ciganos or the "Eastern Line" ("Gypsies"), Crianças or Erês ("children"), Exus and Pombagiras ("scroundels" and "prostitutes"), and Eguns or Sofredores ("wandering souls") (Brumana and Martinez 155–68). Nevertheless, the main, most traditional four types of Umbanda's entidades are Caboclos, Prêtos Velhos, Crianças (Erês), and Exus. These entities are organized into lineages and phalanxes. Pombagiras and Exus also have a strong connection to Eguns, as they are identified with particular persons from the past.

The entities in question include the Pombagira Cigana or Gypsy woman figure who, together with such Exus as Zé Pilintra, represent the *povo da rua* or "street spirits," usually *malandros* ("conmen") and prostitutes (figure 3.11). They dress in red and black, colors of the orixá Exu and the real Gypsies themselves, although white may also be used. In Umbanda, they are considered "lower" or "non-evolved" spirits of "darkness" (*trevas*) or "of the left" (*da esquerda*), who can "evolve" by practicing "charity." It is not surprising to find the voiceless personae of Indians, Old Slaves, Children, Tricksters, as well as Gypsies as the main types of entities in Umbanda, as they reflect the marginality of their worshippers.

As discussed earlier, Umbanda/Quimbanda, with its eclectic and highly ritualized system, is a religion closely linked to liminality through the entities included in the *povo da rua*—Pombagiras

Figure 3.11 *Povo da rua*: Pombagira and Exu, Rio de Janeiro, Brazil, 2009. Photo by author

and Exus—who are also believed to be the most powerful. This is very meaningful for Brazilian society, where a strict division between "house" and "street" exists. While the house is seen as collective, stable, safe, and orderly, the street is perceived as a place of individualization, struggle, movement, and danger, and the living place of rogues, crooks, rascals, and marginals (DaMatta, *A casa & a rua* 55, 57). As discussed earlier, Umbanda includes elements that originated in Kardecist Spiritism, such as the belief in Karmic evolution, the practice of "charity," and direct communication with "guides" or mediums. Spiritism, also called *mesa branca* or "white table," is a more widely accepted possession religion with an intellectual veneer from which African elements have been eliminated, in an attempt to "whiten" the religion and make it more acceptable to middle- and upper-class Brazilians. But even in Umbanda, one can perceive the influence of the dominant, structured society in the divide between the "baptized Exus" that "work for good" and the "pagan" or more African Exus that intervene in black magic and hold the lowermost status. For example, some of the most "evolved" spirits are those from *Linea de Oriente* ("Line of the Orient"), and the African spirits are considered "lower." According to Capone, this stratification mimics the established social order (*A busca* 96–97, 101). Nevertheless, all the entities are interdependent. Umbanda escapes the official, Western-Christian division between "good" and "bad," accepts them both, and works with them equally. A ponto cantado to the "most refined" of Pombagiras, Maria Padilha, reflects this ambiguity:

> She is Maria Padilha
> Who wears the little wooden sandals.
> She works for good,
> But she also works for evil. (Teixeira, *Pomba-Gira: Enchantments*14)

In truth, Afro-Brazilian religions are a complex and dynamic phenomenon, and they can be presented as a continuum, from the least to the most African (table 3.1).[40] Paradoxically, although

Table 3.1 Continuum of Afro-Brazilian religions

Espiritismo (Kardecist Spiritism)	Spiritist doctrine that combines religion, science, and philosophy, created by the Frenchman Allan Kardec in the nineteenth century
"White" Umbanda	Spiritism, also called Mesa Branca ("White Table")
"Africanized" Umbanda	Kardecism with African elements, among others
Omolocô	Religion, considered by many to be extinct, that is similar to Candomblé and includes Umbanda entities
Candombléde C aboclo	Afro-Brazilian religion that includes Native Brazilian elements
Candombléde Angola	Afro-Brazilian religion that includes Bantu elements
CandombléN agô	Afro-Brazilian religion with predominantly Yoruba elements
Re-Africanized Candomblé	Religion claiming African (Yoruba) purity

in the past White Umbanda was the most prestigious of these religions, today it is most chic to belong to Re-Africanized Candomblé with its claims to African purity, which nevertheless is a Brazilian construct, while Umbanda is seen as a syncretic, "impure" religion of the lower classes that combines African, Indian, Catholic, and Spiritist elements.[41]

Origins of Pombagiras: The Yoruban Àwọn Ìyá Wa and the Portuguese *Bruxas*

The Brazilian entity Pombagira is a contemporary example of the demonization of a free female archetype. Her origins go back to Africa, to such divine beings as the Àwọn Ìyá Wa (iyá mis)—the awe-inspiring and powerful ancestral Mothers—and to Spanish and Portuguese Medieval *bruxas* and Galician *meigas*, today seen as "witches,"[42] often burned at stake by the Holy Inquisition, as well as to survival and street life in colonial Brazil, with its need of protection and empowerment of women and the popular classes.

In Yorubaland (Nigeria and Benin), the other main ancestral place for Brazilian traditions, researchers have documented the existence of a mighty feminine force Àjẹ́, "a cosmic force that originates with Great Mother Deities," often misunderstood as "witch." It is "a biological, physical, spiritual force of creativity and social and political enforcement. A vastly influential power that is inclined toward paradox and multiplicity." Àjẹ́ is embodied in the Àwọn Ìyá Wa, Àwọn Ìyàmi Òṣòròngà, as well as in certain persons of power. These powerful ancestral Mothers, also named iyá mi ("my mother"), Ìyàmi ("My Mysterious Mother"), Yewájọbí ("The Mother of All the Òrìṣà and All Living Things"), Àgbàláàgbà ("Old and Wise One"), and Ayé ("The Earth") (Washington 13–14), possess such mystical and dangerous powers—Àjẹ́—that they must be appeased in the Gẹ̀lẹ̀dẹ́ spectacles, through a satirical masquerade:

> Honor to my mother!
> Honor my mother *opake na nake, nake, eeee.*
> *Opake na nake, nake.*
> Mother whose vagina causes fear to all.
> Mother whose pubic hair bundles up in knots.
> Mother who sets a trap, sets a trap.
> Mother who has meat at home in lumps. (Drewal, "Efe" 60)

The performances take place in the main market, a liminal place at the center of the town where roads, human beings, and spirits cross, and which serves as a metaphor for the world. The Mothers, who are the embodiment of power, control the world and the market; they are called *oní l'oní aiyé*, "owners of the world," and "gods of society" (Augras, "De Iyá mi" 18–19; Drewal and Drewal, *Gẹlẹdẹ* 9–11). The dances of Gẹ̀lẹ̀dẹ́ are aimed at placating, pleasing, and pampering the mothers and are performed exclusively by men dressed in women's clothing (Cunha 6). This practice suggests that the great power of the iyá mi must be contained and subdued. It is believed that all women possess Àjẹ́ power, as they are linked to and controlled by the iyá mi through their menstrual blood, and that women are Ẹlẹ́yẹ (Ẹlẹ́iyẹ), "Owners of the Bird" or "Ladies of the Bird," as *ẹyẹ*—bird in a calabash—symbolizes Àjẹ́ (Augras,

"De Iyá mi" 22; Washington 13, 23). Moreover, as Washington contends:

> Selected... Women of Àjẹ́ have many significant attributes and roles in society. They are bestowed with spiritual vision, divine authority, power of the word, and àṣẹ... the power to bring desires and ideas into being. As "children" of Imọlẹ̀, the Mother of the Earth, they control agricultural fertility and plant life. Holistic healing is an important aspect of Àjẹ́, and its wielders use their incomparable knowledge and ownership of flora and fauna to create nourishment, healing elixirs, and poisons. Àjẹ́ also enact spiritual communication through divination and Ọ̀rọ̀, power of the word. (14)

Women and the iyá mi are associated with birds and fish, through their feathers and scales as symbols of multiplication. The Mother is a formidable source of all creation that evokes ambivalence and fright:

> All-powerful mother, mother of the night bird
> Mother who kills animals without striking...
> Great mother with whom we dare not cohabit
> Great mother whose body we dare not see
> Mother of secret beauties
> Mother who empties the cup
> Who speaks out with the voice of a man,
> Large, very large mother on the top of the iroko[43]tree,
> Mother who climbs high and looks down on the earth
> Mother who kills her husband yet pities him. (Beier 10–11)

This Gẹ̀lẹ̀dẹ́ song is reminiscent of the paradoxical Gnostic text "The Thunder, Perfect Mind," where the all-encompassing transcendence of a feminine deity is revealed:

> For I am the first and the last.
> I am the honored and the scorned one.
> I am the whore and the holy one.
> I am the wife and the virgin.
> I am the mother and the daughter...
> I am the barren one

And many are hers ons…
I am the bride and the bridegroom…
For I am knowledge and ignorance.
I am shame and boldness…
I am strength and I am fear…
But I, I am compassionate and I am cruel…
I am the one whom they call life,
And you have called death…
I am control and the uncontrollable.
I am the union and the dissolution.
I, I am sinless,
And the root of sin derives from me…
For I am the one who alone exists,
And I have no one who will judge me. (*The Other Bible* 595–99)

The Sanskrit scripture *Devī-māhātmyam* (Glory of the Divine Mother), describes the great goddess in similar terms:

You are the origin of all the worlds!…You are incomprehensible…This entire world is composed of an infinitesimal portion of yourself! You are verily the supreme primordial Prakrti[44] untransformed. (Ch. 4: 7, 8)

We prostrate before her who is at once most gentle and most terrible; we salute her again and again. Salutation to her who is the support of the world. (Ch. 5: 13)

The Mother from the Gèlèdé song can be described as a liminal being. She is self-sufficient and androgynous, dangerous, and ambivalent—she contains all opposites, she is total and perfect, similar to the absolute transcendence of the feminine divinity from "The Thunder, Perfect Mind," as well as to the descriptions of the Indian Devī, Kālī, who is the incomprehensible "mother" and "origin of all the worlds," who "is at once the most gentle and the most terrible," and "who is essence [and] author of everything" (*Devī-māhātmyam*, Ch. 3: 34; Ch. 4: 7; Ch. 5: 12, 13). Various African-origin myths recount how male gods usurped the great power of the iyá mi ("My Mother" or "Our Mothers"). For example, according to one of them, the chief of religious institutions, Odù, abused her power, which passed under the command of the males, such as the Egungun. The Eguns' role is to maintain social order in the whole of society. This and other myths symbolize the transfer of social power from women to men. Another example is the goddess Nanã who, according to myth, was robbed by the god Oxalá from her exclusive power over the spirits of the dead. Nevertheless, the orixá Iansã/Oyá is still adored as the Queen and Funder of the Egungun secret society, which currently is exclusively male. All the feminine divinities in their archaic form are also iyá mi, and they can assume the form of Ìyàmi Òṣòròngà.[45] The iabás still keep their terrible, indestructible, and powerful Àjẹ́, a taboo word that is substituted by Ẹlẹ́yẹ, "Lady of the Bird," symbolized by a calabash with a bird inside—the great belly, representing female genitive power. Also named Ìyàmi Òṣòròngà, she is the principle of feminine power and chief of all the iyá mi. The archaic essence of the iabás—the feminine orixás of today's Brazil—can be found in Ìyàmi Òṣòròngà (Augras, "De Iyá mi" 22; Capone, *Searching* 60). Both the iyá mi and the Àjẹ́, who are believed to contain large quantities of the vital force, *àṣẹ* (Braz. *axé*), are considered extremely effective and dangerous, similar to the Brazilian Pombagira. In a story from the Ifá corpus, collected by Pierre Verger, it is told how coming to this world, the Ìyàmi-Ẹlẹ́yẹ (Ẹléiyẹ) ("Our Bird-Owning Mothers") perch on seven trees; on three they work for good, on three for evil, and on the seventh – for good and evil alike (Verger 147). In addition, the Àjẹ́ may assume the form of birds, such as doves, pigeons, vultures, and owls (Washington 22). In this context, it is most revealing to remember the Slavic Christmas Carol, discussed in chapter 1, about two doves on an oak tree, who represent the two creators of the world—God and the Devil. In addition, the witch in Western cultures always has a bird companion, usually an owl—a bird of evil—into which she transforms herself at night,[46] while the Virgin Mary and many of her predecessors are often portrayed accompanied by doves. Therefore, the twofold nature of such entities as Exus and Pombagiras, Baba Yaga, Santa Muerte, and Kālī that corresponds to the dichotomy of the world and the truth about the human condition is not surprising. The Gèlèdé festival serves to appease iyá mi's anger, anger that may have an origin in the transfer of control of the Egun society from the female Odù (Ìyàmi) to Obarixá (Orixalá), which symbolizes the shift of social power from women to men.[47] Inf act:

> One of Odù's most significant origin texts [*Ìgbàgbó ati Èṣìn Yorùbá*]...recounts her role in the creation of the earth...Odù was the only woman among the sixteen Òrìṣà that Olódùmarè, the Great Creator, commissioned to make the earth habitable and secure for humanity. Rather than work as a unit, the fifteen males decided to disregard the female principle, Àjẹ́ Odù. With this act, the males rendered themselves biologically and creatively impotent. After integrating Odù in the creative process, the collective instituted life, humanity, ad social structure on earth. In addition to Àjẹ́ being a force essential to creation, the Àjẹ́ of Odù is independent of and complementary to masculine forces...her power surpasses that of the fifteen male Deities...As the descendants of Odù, Àwọn Ìyá Wa inherit the Mother's attributes and continue her struggle against sexual oppression and for holistic harmonization...[Moreover,] Odù... "revealed to [Òrúnmìlà] the knowledge of divination so that man could communicate with the spitit realm"...She endows her daughters, Àwọn Ìyá Wa, with Ọrọ̀a nd Àjẹ́.[48]

Ìyàmi Òṣòròngà, as Pombagira, is also associated with female sexual power, which is complementary to Exu—the symbol of male sexual power. In fact, there is a bond between Exu and the iyá mi; Cunha defines them as "Exu's great-grandmothers" (Capone, *Searching* 61) .

Because of the great and dangerous powers of the iyá mi, as well as the practice of sexual magic by the Portuguese bruxas and other world traditions, the link between these ancient figures and the new Brazilian creation—Pombagira—is not difficult to detect. As Ìyàmi Òṣòròngà, Pombagira is very mighty, and as a liminal persona, she escapes any social rules and restrictions imposed by the structure of patriarchal society. It is enough to remember the universal, paradoxical power of the female deity from "The Thunder, Perfect Mind" who is "the honored and the scorned one," "the whore and the holy one," "the wife and the virgin" (271) to realize that the duality of Pombagira bestows her with extraordinary power, reminiscent of Ìyàmi Òṣòròngà and the Indian Devī. Pombagira appears to embody a submerged and forgotten force, which was, at least formally, eliminated from Brazil with the disappearance of the Gẹ̀lẹ̀dẹ́ festivals by the end of the nineteenth century and the subsequent whitening and domestication of the iabás in White Umbanda. Such is the case of the orixá Iemanjá, who in her public image became an almost ethereal being, subject to national homages and celebrations in Brazil since the 1950s (see figure 3.8).[49]

In Brazil, Sara Kali as well as the sweetened Iemanjá, and of course the Virgin Mary, are more acceptable counterparts to the street woman, she-devil, Pombagira. She is the heir of mighty, independent, self-sufficient female deities with great frightening powers that make them dangerous and may require offerings as well as other means of appeasement. Similar to the figures from different cultures and continents described earlier, Pombagira has a strong connection to sexuality, magic, rage, blood, and death—all attributes of liminality. Like her worshippers, she is an outsider and lives at the periphery of society. She is an extremely marginal entity in today's Brazil, but at the same time the most powerful and fascinating one, as she is endowed with magical powers and is believed to be wise and effective. She "gets things done" without regard for if it is "for good" or "for evil," similar to Mexican Santa Muerte. She dwells in a parallel universe where ambivalent, outsider, trickster entities and the lives of their powerless worshippers are imbued with meaning.

As a "threshold persona," Pombagira lives on the fringes of society, in a contrasting universe, and therefore her transgressions and carnavalizations are uncontrollable. Thus, she fully recuperates her ancient connection to the untamed forces of passion, sexuality, blood, and death of mighty ancient female deities and their representatives. When we hear of murders allegedly perpetrated by Pombagira, such as the ones described by Contins and Goldman, and by Hayes, we are reminded of a line from the ancient Yoruba myth: "Mother that kills her husband yet pities him,"[50] which further reinforces Pombagira's ambivalence. Her strength springs from her lowermost status, from her all-encompassing duality, from the fact that being an outsider frees her from imposed social rules, which she is able to escape. As Michael Taussig affirms, "The gods and the spirits are always and everywhere ambivalent, and the devil is the archsymbol of ambivalence" (230–31).

In the context of the inferior position of the female in most countries of the world, it is significant that the unsubduable, trickster Pombagira entity appeared in nineteenth-century Brazil.[51] Certainly, there are strong and relatively recent antecedents, described earlier, as well as social circumstances of extreme marginality created by over three centuries of slavery, poverty, and an alternative economy, a tradition of a dynamic continuum in syncretic religions, and millions of people currently living in *favelas* ("shantytowns"), places off-limits for the dominant classes, to mention just a few reasons.[52] These marginal individuals often lack basic services and means of subsistence and create alternative, informal, or illegal circuits of earning an income, and of getting physical, emotional, and supernatural help, as in the case of Pombagiras and Exus worship. No matter how many times religions (such as "White Umbanda"), or female divine figures (such as Iemanjá), become literally and metaphorically whitened and dulcified to appear more tamed and "civilized," some sectors of Brazilian society find a way to manifest the lost essence of primordial deities and religious practices, essence that in the majority of cases has already been lost in Yorubaland, where only 20 percent of the population practices the religion of the orixás, with no doubt many innovations compared to Brazil (Cunha 10–11). The ancient function of the holy harlot was easier to be reborn in the liminal circumstances of the excluded. Places with a strongly established

"Western civilization" are usually subject to stronger control, often in overt but also, more dangerously, in covert ways, when people are brought to think they have options and free choice. As a consequence, they may never try to challenge the imposed concepts of culture and to step out of their allowed routine. In spite of appearances, if someone does not conform to the structure of Western society behavior rules, he/she starts being subject to all kinds of repression, first just a social scrutiny and isolation, and later the state and its forces of "law" and "order," or the medical establishment, will do their share. In such a milieu, very few people will put at stake their livelihood, reputation, and social status in order to explore and freely express themselves beyond the established limits. Individuals are not permitted to take justice into their own hands, even in face of blatant and obvious crimes and injustices, not resolved by the authorities. The strong agency of Brazilian Umbanda's Exus and Pombagiras is out to remedy that. As Ruth Landes stated during her 1938–1939 research in Salvador, Bahia, in regard to Candomblé's orixás: "[Exu] is really of more value than the gods because he gets things done...He is ready for service at any time, resting at the cross-roads" ("Fetish" 263):

> He is the master of the street
> With his heavy ceremonies
> Acts in various sectors
> Cemeteries and crossroads
> That's why many times
> Without Exu nothing can be done.[53]

The next chapter focuses on the unofficial saint Santa Muerte that sprung among lower classes of Mexico City in the mid-twentiethc entury.

CHAPTER 4

Santa Muerte, Death the Protector

Dear Death of my heart, don't forsake me from your protection.[1]

Oh Most Holy Death, I invoke you so through your image you may free me from all danger, material or from bewitchment and through this sacred flame you may purify my body from all disgrace and malediction and that in turn love and abundance may come. So be it.

—*La Biblia de la Santa Muerte, n.d. 64*

I don't know if God exists, but death yes...Death is stronger than life, as she puts an end to it. In view of a lack of meaning of life, there is an excess of meaning of death.[2]

The unofficial saint, Santa Muerte or Holy Death, another contemporary manifestation of a fierce liminal deity connected to marginality, inferiority, outsiderhood, and ritual powers, is worshipped in Mexico, Guatemala, Honduras, El Salvador, and the "Greater Mexico" in the United States.[3] This new devotion can be traced to the Tepito neighborhood in Mexico City's marginal *colonia* Morelos, in mid-twentieth century, where it started as a personal cult that spread widely about 20 years ago and reached an unprecedented popularity in the past ten years. In this chapter, I examine the European, Native Mexican, and Colonial origins of the usage of death images and the reasons for the beginning and expansion of Santa Muerte devotion in Mexico and the US-Mexican borderlands, as well as its meaning and implications for individuals and society. Because of the novelty, immediacy, and sometimes clandestine character of this devotion, there is almost no scholarly literature published on this topic, and my sources are my own fieldwork, scarce books, articles, devotional manuals, and the Internet.

Portrayals and Names

Santa Muerte is generally represented as a skeleton wearing a Franciscan monk's cape, in a standing posture (figure 4.1) or sometimes seated on a throne with a scythe in her right hand and the earth or the scale in her left (figure 4.2). She can also carry a candle, a book, or a spade and is often accompanied by an owl, seeds, and coins. A Santa Muerte statue I acquired in 2009 at the Mercado de Sonora in Mexico City, the main esoteric goods market in the country, contains an image of

Figure 4.1 Santa Muerte wearing a Franciscan monk's cape, Piedras Negras, Mexico, 2008. Photo by author

Figure 4.2 Santa Muerte seated on a throne, San Antonio, United States, 2012. Photo by author

Jesus on the cross, the Holy Ghost as a dove, pieces of gold, a lucky four-petal trefoil, and a horseshoe. Her scythe is adorned by a skull and a rose. Following the baroque, overabundance logic of syncretic devotions, the more superimposed symbols an object contains, the greater its power, as it is believed that it accumulates the energies of all traditions involved. Variations of Santa Muerte's outfit include a Virgin Mary–like robe and veil, a girl's first communion dress or a bride's gown (figure 4.3), a China Poblana outfit, an "Aztec" Santa Muerte (figure 4.4), and a seven-colored one (figure 4.5), among others, depending on the occasion and the petition. On some images, her scythe is portrayed in the form of a human spine. In addition, since the 1990s, some younger people started to create artistic representations of Santa Muerte, inspired in horror movies and heavy metal (Roush 145). This fluidity and flexibility of her

Figure 4.3 Santa Muerte wearing a bride's gown, Mercado de Sonora, Mexico City, 2009. Photo by author

representations reflects the fact that she eludes official circuits of Church and State and is only subject to individual needs and creativity. In addition, public altars have special persons in charge of caring for this figure and often have godfathers or godmothers (*padrinos* or *madrinas*) that support them. They are regularly cleaned and renewed, and La Flaquita's ("The Skinny One's") clothes are changed every month, as the Virgin Mary's robes are changed in the Catholic tradition, and are subject to the imagination of her devotees. La Santita ("The Little Saint") is often adorned with long hair, jewelry, a crown, and in some places there is a tendency to her softening, as in the Iglesia Tridentina of self-proclaimed archbishop Romo, where she was renamed as "The Angel of Death" ("El Angel de la Muerte"),[4] or by the influence of Santería in Veracruz, where her image

Figure 4.4 "Aztec" Santa Muerte, San Antonio, United States, 2012. Photo by author

is sometimes merged with that of the *orixá/oricha* or goddess Iemanjá/Yemayá from Brazilian Umbanda/Cuban Santería religions[5] (see figure 3.8). In this case, Santa Muerte is portrayed as a beautiful, young, white woman, called "The White Flower of the Universe" ("La Flor Blanca del Universo") or "The Young Encarnated Death" ("La Joven Muerte Encarnada") (Flores, "Transformismos"63) .

Offerings to Santa Muerte include *veladoras* ("votive candles"; figure 4.6) statuettes, flowers, incense, fruits, sweets, smoking cigars and cigarettes, as well as alcohol, such as tequila, rum, and whiskey. Devotees often blow tobacco smoke on her as a sign of blessing and kiss and touch her glass case at Enriqueta Romero's altar in Mexico City's Tepito neighborhood. If they are lucky, they can also touch her robe from an open side. These rituals, as well as the main two colors—red and black—evoke another

Figure 4.5 Seven-colored Santa Muerte, San Antonio, United States, 2012. Photo by author

unofficial devotion—that of the Roma at the Saint Sara-La-Kâli subterranean altar at Les Saintes Maries-de-la-Mer in southern France (see figure 2.2)[6]; the cigars and alcohol, as well as the colors, are reminiscent of Pombagira from the Umbanda religion in Brazil, discussed in chapter 3. Santa Muerte is portrayed in various forms and colors that have symbolic significance and are connected to the intention of the person's offering. She is also called a myriad of different names, a powerful testament to the special relationship between her and her devotees.[7] Usually she is represented by a statuette or even a human-size statue, a candle, an *escapulario* ("scapular"), medallion, ring, bracelet, or tattoo; she appears on paintings and graffiti, as well as on various products, such as T-shirts, incense, perfumes, oils, and soaps (figure 4.7). Her statue can be made of diverse materials,[8] and her colors may be red—for love, passion, and relationships;

Figure 4.6 Santa Muerte *veladora*, San Antonio, United States, 2012. Photo by author

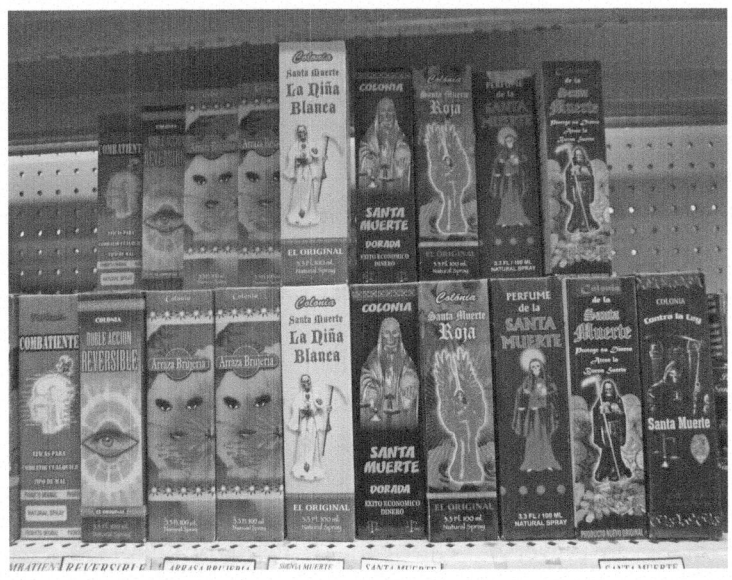

Figure 4.7 Santa Muerte products, Botánica Papa Jim's, San Antonio, United States, 2012. Photo by author

Figure 4.8 Santa Muerte covered in dollar bills, Mercado de Sonora, Mexico, 2009. Photo by author

white—for purification; black—for and against black magic, the elimination of negativity, and total protection; violet—for health and transmutation; gold or yellow—for money and prosperity; blue—for spiritual concentration and studies; and green—for legal problems and justice. There are also variations, such as a Santa Muerte fully covered in dollar bills (figure 4.8), La Niña Blanca ("The White Girl") as the Virgin of Guadalupe (figure 4.9), and other "new" colors, such as amber—for the healing of drug addictions and alcoholism; brown—for enlightenment and wisdom; and rose—for romance. Popular are also seven-colored images and candles that encompass all of these attributes, called La Santa Muerte de los Siete Poderes ("Saint Death of the Seven Powers") (Guttman 21; Perdigón 92–93) or Las Siete Muertes ("Seven Deaths"), that offer powers embodied in the different color energies that have a positive effect on work,

Figure 4.9 Santa Muerte as the Virgin of Guadalupe, cover, *La biblia de la Santa Muerte* (n.d.). Photo by author

health, loyalty, understanding, fortune, and forgiveness. On a "made-in-Mexico" votive candle I acquired at a San Antonio *botánica* ("religious store"), the disposition of six different colored La Flaquita images placed around a main one called "Santa Muerte" evokes a visual arrangement from Santería. These new Santa Muerte candles are most likely derived from the notion of Las Siete Potencias Africanas ("Seven African Powers") from Afro-Cuban Santería, which portray seven saints syncretized with seven orichas or African Yoruba gods, namely, Changó, Ochún, Yemayá, Obatalá, Orula, Ogún, Eleguá, placed around JesusC hristor Olof i.

Methods of Devotion and Devotees

In Texas, Santería candles and other unofficial saints' candles, such as Niño Fidencio's and even the "Reverse" black and red candle, can be bought at any botánica or a Hispanic neighborhood *bodega* ("grocery store"). For a while, Santa Muerte candles were also sold at the giant supermarket chain HEB, but they have been removed from the latter, probably because she is viewed negatively by the general public. Although some of her characteristics are rather stable, Santa Muerte is the focus of a living cult and, like other popular syncretic devotional figures and practices, she is multivalent and in constant flux. Therefore, her attributes may change from place to place and from time to time, as she is a depositary of human creativity and changing social circumstances and reflects the transcient nature of her worshippers. Devotees have appropriated La Santa Muerte to serve them in the way they want to be served, rather than obeying a fixed prescription imposed from above, which constitutes one of her appeals. If the Santita ("Little Saint") does not fulfill their wishes, she may be punished by being placed upside down, buried, or by having her hand taken away until she fulfills the devotee's wishes, as other colonial saint statues were and continue to be treated by the populace.[9] This may also be the reason why Doña Enriqueta's center in Mexico City was more popular than that of self-proclaimed archbishop David Romo Guillén, who allegedly tried to institutionalize and centralize La Santísima's devotion by creating a corrupt hierarchy and an intent to build a cathedral for her. Nevertheless, Santa Muerte's devotees favor a direct and spontaneous relation with their saint, who does not need mediators, hierarchy, or authority (Martín 207–208). In spite of their fervent devotion to La Señora Blanca ("The White Lady"), the majority of Santa Muertistas consider themselves Roman Catholic, and they incorporate Santa Muerte in their devotion as another saint, albeit the most powerful. They also tend to worship San Judas Tadeo and the Virgin of Guadalupe, but consider Santa Muerte to be much stronger (Osorno 183, 188). Keeping with her mediating role, she is often considered the Angel of God, the Messenger of God, His Wife, or the Holy Spirit, and her images and chapels are placed on Mexican street corners and highways. However, the Catholic hierarchy does not accept the devotion to Santa Muerte as part of their faith. We have to remember that, like many Latin American religions, the Santa Muerte devotion is syncretic and borrows heavily from Catholicism, as well as from other, unorthodox cults. This is visible in the liturgy that follows the Catholic model. The rosaries, masses, altars, and prayers for her are modeled on and accompanied by Catholic prayers, such as Hail Mary, Our Father, and Glory Be.[10] Her altars may be fixed, like those in households, businesses, penitentiaries, and on the streets, or they may be mobile, as in the case of ambulant vendors, *carros de la muerte* ("chariots of death"), vans, trucks, buses, or taxis. On the altars she may appear alone, or accompanied by Jesus, the Virgin Mary, the Buddha, or an owl, among others (Perdigón 80–81). In addition, as a border saint, she is liminal par excellence, as she trespasses official control reflecting the transgressive status of her devotees, such as migrants or criminals. A striking symbol of this transciency and temporality are the dozens of Santa Muerte shrines erected and subsequently destroyed, along the freeways linking the border area cities of Monterrey, Reynosa, and Nuevo Laredo (Martín 4; Osorno 188; "Santa Muerte, 'narcoaltares'").

Although Santa Muerte acquired a negative image in the media, as a pseudo-saint of *narcotraficantes* ("drug traffickers") and other delinquents, her devotion is very widely spread among ordinary mortals, such as housewives and other working people, most of whom feel abandoned by official Church and State. Nevertheless, her bad name requires a separate mention, as she is also found on *narcoaltares* ("drug altars") belonging to high-profile drug traffickers. She is presented in such a role in Homero Aridjis's novel *La Santa Muerte*, which describes the fiftieth birthday celebration of a Mexican capo. In the book, there is one chapter devoted to a Santa Muerte ceremony where, beside drug traffickers, ecclesiastical, civil, and army dignitaries as well as entertainment world stars are present, and which includes human sacrifice. Although this type of manifestation is the one that can most often be found in sensationalistic press articles, TV news, or soap operas, this does not constitute the main aspect of the devotion, which is widespread, individual, and spontaneous and pertains to people from all walks of life.

Devotional Centers, Transnationality, and Scope

Until David Romo's arrest and his convictions in 2011 and 2012 (see note #4), among thousands of places of worship, there were two main focal points of the cult in Mexico City, both in the marginal *colonia* Morelos. One in the Tepito neighborhood, in front of the home of Enriqueta (Queta) Romero on 12 Alfarería Street, where she first publicly displayed a life-size statue of La Santísima in 2001 and started a communal prayer service that developed into a monthly rosary ceremony (Roush 132–33; Chesnut 12–13); and the other at the Iglesia Tradicional México-Estados Unidos, Misioneros del Sagrado Corazón y San Felipe de Jesús, at 35 Nicolás Bravo Street, led by its self-proclaimed archbishop David Romo, where Santa Muerte was called Angel de Luz ("Angel of Light"), Angel de Dios ("Angel of God"), Angel de la Muerte ("Angel of Death"), and Amabilísima Madre ("Most Kind Mother"), among others. In this center, masses, rosaries, pilgrimages, as well as weddings, baptisms, and confirmations were performed. They also established the first national holiday devoted to Saint Death on August 15, the same day when Catholics celebrate the important feast of the Assumption of the Virgin Mary. The Mexican Secretaría de Gobernación (Ministry of the Interior) revoked the permit from this church in 2005, alleging that they deviated from their original goals, perpetrating infractions to the Religious Associations Law. Both centers professed the adoration of Santa Muerte, but they approached it in different ways. The Parroquia de la Misericordia followed the Trent Holy Mass established by Pope Pio V, which was abandoned by the Catholic Church in 1969, after the Second Vatican Council. This devotion differed in some aspects from the doctrine of the Roman Catholic Church and was not accepted by it, as since 2002 the Iglesia Tradicional included Santa Muerte worship (Perdigón 108–109, 114, 117). According to Enriqueta Romero, in 2010, there were 1,500 altars to Santa Muerte in Mexico City alone, and David Romo asserted that there were 10 million Santa Muerte devotees. Besides these two centers of devotion, all of Mexico and the borders between Mexico and other countries to the north and south also have many places of worship of La Santísima. For example, in 2007 the largest (22-meter-tall) public Santa Muerte statue was erected in Taltitlán, central Mexico. This statue, which is accompanied by an altar and a store, has become a place of devotion and pilgrimage from both sides of the border.[11]

Santa Muerte's omnipresence has been reinforced by the transnational migrations and by the electronic media, pertinent to the postmodern world in which she emerged. Her cult is mostly individual and heterogeneous, but in Mexico it is also subject to abundant public displays, including statues, shrines, altars, and chapels. It is also highly commercialized; I was recently surprised during a visit to the Botánica Papa Jim's, a huge religious goods supermarket in the Hispanic West Side neighborhood of San Antonio, Texas, to find Santa Muerte statues and candles dominating the space among the myriad of aisles with different products. Her representations included a central altar with a seated La Madrina statue where diverse offerings were placed. In contrast, there were only a few small Virgin of Guadalupe icons, not very visible to the public (figure 4.10). I found a similar situation in other religious stores in San Antonio that include La Hermana Blanca, such as *Botánica Elegguá*, and in San Cristóbal de las Casas, Mexico (figure 4.11).

Conversely, during my fieldwork in San Antonio botánicas 15 years ago, I did not notice any Santa Muerte images or items, and the Virgin of Guadalupe was the main icon displayed. Besides selling products, these stores also offer esoteric services of various natures, from *limpias* ("cleansings") by *curanderos* to tarot and Santería's Dillogún readings and Palo Mayombe

Figure 4.10 Santa Muerte and Guadalupe, Botánica Papa Jim's, San Antonio, United States, 2012. Photo by author

rituals. Different kinds of items and services are offered in the same place, which may lead to syncretic mixtures. Santa Muerte devotees usually consider themselves Catholic or Santeros[12] and practice a combination of different rituals. Nevertheless, not all of San Antonio botánicas include Santa Muerte.[13]

What is the reason for such quickly spreading devotion to this peculiar figure? The cult of Santa Muerte, like other unofficial devotions, such as the ones to Niño Fidencio, Pedrito Jaramillo, or Jesús Malverde, is directly related to poverty, marginality, and conflict. The difference with La Jefa ("The Boss") is that while the aforementioned folk cults are based on historical or legendary individuals, the personalized, feminine Santa Muerte, on the other hand, is a symbolic, all-encompassing figure. She is invoked for protection and strength, in the hope of transforming disorder into order in the private lives of often vulnerable individuals, their families, and their communities. Devotees ask

Figure 4.11 Santa Muerte and Guadalupe, botánica, San Cristóbal de las Casas, Mexico, 2014. Photo by author

her for employment, prosperity, good health, love, and protection from enemies or rivals. The following poem of thanks to La Niña Blanca resumes the meaning she has for devotees:

> You have become a very special being in my life
> I think about you every instant and my faith in you grows
> Since I know you I don't feel alone anymore
> I know that God sent you to me so I can ask you with great love
> You want the best for your sons and daughters and you know what is in our hearts
> So my girl you already know well mine
> You know everything about me, you know all my needs and that's why I ask you with great love
> I carry you in my heart forever.[14]

As it has been noted before, the devotion to La Señora Blanca started to be widespread in Mexico City in the early 1990s, especially in domestic altars of the precarious Tepito neighborhood, among persons at the fringes of society who by their liminal occupations were exposed to danger and death. This included street vendors, prostitutes, criminals, inmates, homosexuals, and transgendered individuals, but later spread to many other occupations that deal with transitions, transgressions, such as migrants, truck and taxi drivers, policemen, troops, prison guards, psychologists, and lawyers, and the middle class. It is also a cult directly related to drug trafficking, as its members daily commingle with danger and death. In this case, her powers may also be used to harm enemies or rivals in the trade. Devotees of Santa Muerte have often been stigmatized as *narcosatáticos* ("narco-satanic"),[15] nevertheless the great majority of them are regular citizens of diverse backgrounds, and it can be argued that Santa Muerte is menacing for the official social structures, such as the government and the Catholic and the Evangelical Churches because she " fills a void in the face of the failure of civil society and the state for those on the margins, especially migrants, impoverished barrio dwellers, and most contentiously, for criminals, to establish alternative forms of spatial and temporal communities, commerce or trade, and social services through secular sanctity" (Martín 185).

Death and Contemporary Mexican Society

The Mexican devotion to death has ancient roots related to human insecurity in the face of such uncontrollable events as illness and massive death because of epidemics, wars, and catastrophes, and was well-developed in Catholic and Native Mexican beliefs before the La Santísima phenomenon took hold.[16] What is most significant though is that death's new avatar, Santa Muerte, emerged in contemporary times, in the mid-twentieth century; she is coded as feminine; and beginning ten years ago, she has enjoyed an unprecedented popularity among wide sectors of the population in Mexico and among its neighbors north and south of the border. What are the reasons for this surprising phenomenon, especially taking into consideration that Mexico already had its protective saint-queen in the figure of the Virgin of Guadalupe? Multiple devotees report that traditional Catholic saints, such as the Virgin of Guadalupe and San Judas Tadeo, are currently not enough, and they need a more efficient and independent figure, such as La Huesuda ("The Bony One"). According to the Catholic informant Angélica López, "I had asked the same favor of Saint Judas Tadeo and the Virgin of Guadalupe, but they didn't help me. A friend told me to require it of Santa Muerte, and she did help me" (Osorno 183). Although the population of Latin America, specially the Indians and the imported black slaves, has been subject to all kinds of mistreatment, hardships, and even massive death since colonial times, and as a consequence developed many survival strategies including popular devotions, it is also true that such a fast and massive growth of a particular cult is uncommon. Nevertheless, when we examine the lucrative movement of the drug traffic from Latin America to the United States, which passes through the Mexican border in these globalized times, especially since the opening of Mexico to international markets and the Free Trade Agreement (NAFTA), signed on January 1, 1994, and later developments such as the "War on Drugs" proclaimed by President Calderón, war that claimed an astounding number of over 65,000 victims in the six years of his presidency (2006–2012),[17] we start to see a larger picture of a country caught up in the middle of an extended, unstable, liminal period of war that hardly anyone is immune to.[18] The economic crisis, known as "the tequila effect" ("el efecto tequila"), that accompanied the transition from the Carlos Salinas de Gortari (1988–1994) to the Ernesto Zedillo (1994–2000) government reduced the buying power of the middle class by 200 percent compared to 1970 levels and provoked a wave of insecurity and violence in the country (Gil 92). In fact, this crisis encompasses the entire population, including politicians, famous artists, and sports figures. From criminals, troops, police, and special-forces to small commerce and the service industry that suffers the consequences of the drop in tourism, great numbers of people have had their livelihoods threatened. A striking reflection of this situation is the "necrophiliac esthetics" of Teresa Margolles, who shocked the audience of the 53rd Venice Biennale with her forensic art pieces, such as *Lengua* (*Tongue*), presenting an actual pierced tongue of a young victim, and *Entierro* (*Burial*) in which she utilized tattoos from actual cadavers. She used to steal materials from a Mexico City morgue, but now they can be readily found on the streets. Her work is an example of continuity and alteration in the Mexican tradition of *Memento Mori*, discussed further in this chapter.[19] Other artists, such as Lenin Márquez, also report an urgency to document the everyday violence that surrounds them.[20] In earlier chapters, I examined the sacred symbolism of the fragmentation of the human body, in regard to divinities such as Baba Yaga and Kālī. The above scattered fragments, on the other hand, indicate interrupted existence, cut short by extreme violence. Although the imagery may be similar, the social meaning is quite antithetical. While in the case of the goddesses it indicates wholeness of opposites, here it points out to broken, truncated lives in the most literal sense.

Like La Pelona ("The Bald One"), who is a dual, ambiguous figure in Western terms—neither good nor bad—her devotees can also find themselves in an ambivalent and contradictory position, crossing borders, switching sides, or collaborating with both, as in the case of "agents of order" that work together with organized crime. I see Santa Muerte devotion as the last recourse, after everything else, including the government and religion with its protectors, such as God, Jesus, and the emblematic Virgin of Guadalupe, has failed. In fact, in spite of her appropriation by some groups of the population,[21] Guadalupe is still seen by many as a symbol of religious orthodoxy, while Santa Muerte, like La Llorona, is the patron of the dispossessed.[22] As one of my informants put it, "Santa Muerte carries out things for you that the Virgin of Guadalupe can't."[23]

A prayer that goes back to mid-twentieth-century-Tepito, states:

> Santísima Muerte, we believe in you because we know that you have existed since the beginning of time.
> We believe in you because you are fair, and do not discriminate. You take a young person just as you take an old person, a rich person just as a poor person.
> We believe in you, because you are the mother of all cycles.
> (Roush13 4)

The insecurity, fragility, ambiguity, and anguish about the lack of legal, economic, and social justice in everyday life, experienced by millions of people in modern Mexican society, give rise to the need for a strong, impartial, and fearless advocate, such as La Madrina, who will protect and defend them from the unpredictability of sudden attacks, kidnappings, stray bullets, arrests, violence, addiction, illness, hunger, and ruin and who is *on their side* and accepts them no matter the social class, sexual orientation, race, or legal status. As other syncretic cults of Latin America, Santa Muerte represents the transgression of boundaries and is a spontaneous, utilitarian devotion geared toward everyday protection and help in difficult life situations, a sort of saint of last resorts. In view of the failure of the state and the judicial system to protect citizens and provide possibilities for their well-being, Santa Muerte "catalyzes social discontent, 'corrects the uncertainty' and re-constructs the social fabric that was lost with the crisis of the State" (Gil 151). As various other attitudes of different Latin American peoples in the face of aggression and difficulty, such as mockery, irony, play, or passive resistance, the devotion to La Niña Blanca is another survival strategy vis-a-vis tremendous life strides. It is enough to consult any Santa Muerte devotional book[24] to realize that the prayers, rituals, and *amarres* ("binding spells") are not geared toward an abstract salvation of the soul, but to everyday survival in all areas of daily life. A good example is "Una oración para invocar" ("A Prayer to Invoke [Santa Muerte]"):

> Ladyof de ath
> Skeletals pirit
> Most powerful and strong,
> Indispensable in the moment of danger,
> I invoke you certain of your bounty.
> Beg to omnipotent god,
> Grant me all I am asking for.
> Make repent all his life
> The one who harmed me or gave me the evil eye
> And may it turn against him right away.
> For the one who deceives me in love
> I ask that you make him come back to me
> And if he does not listen to your strange voice
> Good spirit of death,
> Make him feel
> The power of your scythe.
> In games and in business
> My best advocate I name you
> And anyone that comes against me
> Make him a loser.
> Oh, Lady of Death, my protecting angel, amen! (*La Biblia de la Santa Muerte*, n.d.:36)

In this invocation to La Señora de la Muerte, questions of danger, witchcraft, love, business, and good luck in gambling are included, all areas impossible to control by her devotees. Other prayers from *La Biblia de la Santa Muerte* serve to counteract a whole gamut of specific problems that may occur in a devotee's daily life.[25] These prayers, as well as *trabajos* or "works"—rituals geared toward the attainment of a goal—deal with every possible life affliction, including getting rid of evil spells and freeing oneself from debt or making someone repay a debt. While prayers are petitions on a verbal level that may include some limited actions, rituals involve material objects, specific actions and words, specific days and hours of the week, and are usually repetitive and extended in time. It is expected that a ritual for a singular problem that involves symbolic actions and several senses is more efficacious than mere words. In addition, special altars for homes and specific places, such as a business, a restaurant, or a legal office, are a common practice in Mexico. They usually include a color-specific Santa Muerte statue, a votive candle, a glass of water, flowers, fruits, cigarettes, incense, and alcohol, among other symbolic objects. With individual and collective prayers such as novenas and rosaries, rituals, altars, and worn objects, the life of a devotee in Mexico City is encompassed by their worship of Santa Muerte.[26] The prevalence of her scapulars, medallions, and tattoos, as an ultimate shield and identity symbol worn on the body, speaks to the great need for protection and help. In spite of three centuries of colonial rule of slavery and forced labor since the sixteenth century, it seems that Mexico has never experienced a crisis encompassing every social class on every level of existence, such as the one unfolding in the twenty-first century. Santa Muerte, a liminal saint that characteristically emerged at a time of a socioeconomic conjuncture that encompasses the entire population, stands as a mute, albeit not passive, witness to this predicament. Although it is true that images of death have accompanied various societies for centuries, as described later, what is most surprising is that today La Santísima does not only remind people of their mortality, but she represents their only certainty. Therefore, she has become the most trusted agent of protection of the livelihoods for millions of people. This includes the paradox of Lady Death being recurred to in works against bullets, illness, and for good health, which are meant to prolong life.

Historical Antecedents

From a historical perspective, Santa Muerte has many antecedents manifested in world cultures that created their own representations, beliefs, and rituals connected to death. One of the beliefs is that of the afterlife, common to all religions, in which death is "softened" through the conviction that life will continue, either in heaven (or hell) or in other incarnations on earth. These beliefs have been accompanied by iconographic representations and rituals geared to assure immortality. An example is mummification, where many peoples all over the world, from Egypt to Peru, preserved their dead bodies, so the soul could have a place to return. The memory of deceased noble individuals was preserved through elaborate tombs and pyramids, as well as reenacted in processions where the dead individual was impersonated by a substitute called *wauje* or "brother," as in ancient Inca and pre-Inca cultures. Catholicism propagated the dogma of Christ's passion as victory over death, which was inflicted on mankind when God punished Adam and Eve with their expulsion from Paradise. In iconography, the mortality of all people was depicted in the form of a skull with two crossed femurs, which was placed under every cross. It symbolized "the triumph of the Holy Cross over Death" and the *Memento Mori* ("Remember that You Will Die") (Malvido, "Crónicas" 22). The Catholic Church disseminated the idea of the Good Death or the Holy Death, which could be attained by practicing the seven sacraments of baptism, confirmation, Eucharist, confession, anointment of the sick, the priestly order, and matrimony. Additionally, this *vivir bien* or "good living" was accompanied by death rituals, such as the Holy Communion, the holy anointment on the eve of death, and burial in holy places, among others (Perdigón 24). Sisterhoods, brotherhoods, and congregations were formed,[27] murals were painted in churches, and treatises about the *Ars Morendi* ("the Art of Dying") were written to reinforce this idea against the Mala Muerte or "Bad Death," which meant sudden death without the proper sacraments and a proper burial in sacred ground (Malvido, "Crónicas" 22; Navarrete 19). These rituals were geared toward the attainment of immortality in heaven. Contemporary attempts to prolong youth setting death apart are performed through the manipulation of the body or face by means of cosmetic surgery, various creams and hormonal treatments; injections of embryonic cells; and even freezing of the body until science advances to the point that it can extend life. The overvalorization of "commodities"—accumulation of possessions, extreme overconsumption, and grasping—can also be seen as a way of denying death.[28]

The European Middle Ages, a time directly preceding the Spanish and Portuguese colonization of the Americas, constituted a tremendous encounter with death for members of every social class, as a consequence of the plague known as the "black death" (1347–1349), which killed 80 percent of the population of that continent in the fourteenth century. As a consequence, graphic images of death, such as the "Triumphs of Death" ("Los triunfos de la muerte") and the "Dance of Death" ("Danza macabra"), which depicted a semi-emaciated death dancing with persons from different social strata, abounded in medieval churches and cemeteries. This imagery spread to all arts (Malvido, "Crónicas" 24–25), symbolizing that death is everywhere and spares nobody.[29] This equalizing power of death is one of the reasons why her images become so popular in liminal times of danger and crisis.

In the colony of New Spain (Mexico and part of Central America), where 80 percent of the population died as a consequence of various pandemics in the sixteenth–eighteenth centuries, death became an ever present persona in life and art, from painting, sculpture, architecture, literature to theatre, dance, and processions. Ways of representing her went from a simple skull, often with femurs, to a full skeleton with a crown and scythe or arch and quiver. The symbols of death that spread out in Europe during the Renaissance and are still present in Santa Muerte images, such as the skeleton with a scythe, the bat, the owl, the sand clock, the distaff with the cut thread and a spindle on the floor, originated mostly in pagan art. Among the structures circulating through the streets of New Spain were the *carretas* and *carretones de la muerte* or "death chariots." They were composed of a skeleton of death crowned and enthroned, holding a scythe. This image was used in the Holy Friday processions to represent the triumph of death over Christ. He in turn would conquer death as he resurrected three days later. Similar carts are used today to transport statues of La Santa Muerte trough Mexico City streets. Because of this omnipresence of death imagery in colonial Mexico, it is not surprising that, according to church documents, already in 1797, Indians in San Luis de Paz, Guanajuato, adored a skeletal figure whom they called "Santa Muerte."[30]

In today's Mexico, there still exist at least three skeletal representations of colonial origin. The first one, San Pascualito Rey o San Pascual Bailón from Tuxtla Gutiérrez, Chiapas, seems to have originated in 1650 Guatemala after the end of the epidemic, with an image that was called San Pascual Bailón or San Pascual Rey.[31] The second, Nuestra Señora, la Muerte or la Santa Muerte from Yanhuitlán, Oaxaca, represented as an enthroned and crowned skeleton with a scythe and a candle, seated on a mobile card, probably from the eighteenth century, was placed in the chapel of the town church until 1960 and currently is housed in the museum adjacent to the church. Today, this image receives many pilgrims that venerate La Santa Muerte. A similar image is La Canina, still used in the Holy Week processions in Seville, Spain. The third Mexican image, San Bernardo or Santa Muerte from the Catholic Church of Saint Augustine in Tepatepec, Hidalgo, is the object of veneration of pilgrims from Mexico and as far as Brazil and the United States. This figure is a robed, wooden skeleton seated with a crown and scepter. In addition, among cases denounced by the Inquisition in 1793 was the idol named Justo Juez ("Just Judge"). It was the Muerte Flechadora or "Archer Death," also called Muerte Peste or "Plague Death," represented as a seated skeleton with an arch and arrows. These images were forbidden and their public display was persecuted by the church, especially since the second half of the eighteenth century (Perdigón 31–34; Tavárez 43). This practice was reinforced after the creation of a Mexican secular state in the nineteenth century.

Nevertheless, the earlier representations subsisted clandestinely until the twentieth century when they were reborn in the form of a new cult—that of "Holy Death" or Santa Muerte, name given previously by Native Mexicans to some of the images described earlier. Moreover, Mexico and Guatemala are not the only Latin American countries that venerate a skeletal image. San la Muerte portrayed as a standing caped masculine skeleton holding a scythe, from the Argentine province of Corrientes and possibly of Guaraní Indian origin, worshipped today in Argentina and Paraguay, is a similar image. Interestingly, this figure, for which red and black candles are lit, is said to be associated with the Afro-Brazilian entity, Exu (Perdigón 34, 122–34), a mediator god who is neither good nor bad and is symbolized by red and black colors, discussed in chapter 3.

Although they brought these images to the Americas, European colonizers were not the only ones concerned with death. The ancient Mexicas or Aztecs venerated Mictlantecuhtli and Mictecacíhuatl, the Lord and the Lady of Death, who inhabited the subterranean world, Mictlan. Skulls and other symbols of death were prominently featured in Middle American cultures, for example, in the iconography of goddesses such as Coatlicue (see figure I.1), the Cihuateteo (figure 4.12),[32] and in the *tzompantlis* or walls full of sculls representing sacrificed victims, which can still be seen in Mexico today. One of the oldest Middle American representations of death is a clay mask on which the right side is a normal human face and the left one is skeletal, from the Pre-Classical (1800–0 BC) Tlatilco; it shows the duality of life and death, so important for pre-Columbian peoples. Similar representations, including sculptures with a live individual on one side and a dead one on the other, are common in Middle American native cultures (see Matos, *Artes de México* 6, 24). In fact, Native Mexican societies were keenly aware of death, rebirth, and the passage of time, which is expressed by

Figure 4.12 Cihuateteo, Mexico City. Photo by author

their elaborate and precise calendar system.[33] The concept of the constant flux of life and death is verbalized in the following Nahuatl poems:

> Does one truly live on earth?
> Not forever on earth: Only a little here.
> Although from jade it brakes,
> although from gold it tears up
> although quetzal's plumage it splits,
> not forever on earth: Only a little here.[34]
> and
> We only come to sleep,
> we only come to dream:
> It is not true, it is not true
> that we come to live on earth!...
> Our body produces some flowers
> and there it remains withered. [35]

Death in Mexican Arts and Folklore

From the conflation of European and Middle American traditions that emphasized death and featured it prominently in their arts, as well as from the fact that the colony of New Spain's population was decimated by severe epidemics, we can easily say that Mexicans have continuously been accompanied by representations of death in their daily lives. This in spite of the prohibitions to display such images by the Catholic Church since the eighteenth century and of public manifestations of faith by the state since Leyes de Reforma (1859–1863) in the nineteenth century (Perdigón 31–36). This ubiquitous presence of death permeated the society and manifested in various creative ways as well, such as the caricaturesque engravings of José Guadalupe Posada (1852–1913) who created the figure of La Calavera Catrina ("Elegant Lady") and whom Diego Rivera

Figure 4.13 Altar for the Dead, San Antonio, United States, 2012. Photo by author

later retook as a caricature of a wife of a dignitary parading as a skeleton dressed in a hat and high-society clothes, in his *Sueño de una tarde dominical en la Alameda Central*. Posada used the *calavera* or image of death in many engravings in a burlesque way, as a means of social critique. In the 1930s, during the presidency of Lázaro Cárdenas, intellectuals created many Mexican identity myths, including "the Mexican's play, disregard, making fun of death" (Malvido, "El mexicano" 101). Posada's Catrina figure became part of Mexican folklore, and it is very common to see her today mixed in on Altars for the Dead and even with Santa Muerte images.

The Altars for the Dead constitute a Mexican tradition of honoring the departed with sacred spaces that include *cempazuchitl* ("marigold"), *pan de muerto* ("bread of the dead"), photographs of the deceased, as well as their favorite food and drink, flowers, candles, and La Catrina images (figure 4.13).

Figure 4.14 Lowrider, Lowrider Festival, San Antonio, United States, 2012. Photo by author

These altars can be seen all over Mexico and in many cities in the United States, such as San Antonio, Chicago, and Los Angeles. A recent variation, observed in San Antonio, Texas, is the *lowrider trunk altars*, which continue a Mexican American tradition of creating elaborate vehicles that include murals, luxurious upholstery, hydraulics, and lacquer jobs (figure 4.14) but this time with Altars for the Dead in their trunks. Among the trunk Altars of the Dead I observed in the Centro Cultural Aztlán in San Antonio, on October 2, 2012, there was a particular one that featured images of La Santa Muerte (figure 4.15). The flexibility and fluidity of Mexican American folk traditions is obvious in the adaptation of the Altars of the Dead to lowrider car trunks as well as in the incorporation of new popular icons, such as Santa Muerte. Customarily, the Altars for the Dead were arranged as table-altars. We are now witnessing the merging of two separate traditions—that of lowriders and that of the Altars

Figure 4.15 Lowrider trunk altar for the dead with Santa Muerte, Centro Cultural Aztlán, San Antonio, United States, 2012. Photo by author

for the Dead that includes unprecedented images, such as the one of Santa Muerte. There is also the custom of entire families gathering at the graves of their departed on November 1, the All Saints Day, and November 2, the Day of the Dead, bringing food and drink and "sharing it" with the dead. This practice is not unique to Native Mexicans, as the Roma and other world cultures have similar customs. In this context, commemorating the dead is not a new, sad, or solemn occasion, but rather a happy one, as it is believed that the departed are present and that they accompany the community on that day.[36]

Santa Muerte, Pombagira, and the History of Latin America

Both Pombagira and Santa Muerte appeared in their present forms in the twentieth century at times of socioeconomic crises, among marginal populations, in areas of Latin America that used to be centers of colonial power, the Portuguese Captaincy Colonies of Brazil, and the Spanish Viceroyalty of New Spain, respectively, and have strong antecedents in ancient and colonial devotions. Those antecedents are African and Portuguese in the case of Pombagira and Native Mexican and Spanish in the case of Santa Muerte. The spells these figures perform go back to the magic of the Iberian *bruxas*, as well as to the African Àjẹ́, and the Native American shamans. For example, a prayer to Pombagira says:

> My Queen Pomba Gira Maria Pahilha of the Seven Crossroads, go wherever (name) and don't let him rest, don't let him sleep, don't let him talk, don't let him be cheerful, don't let him feel pleasure until he talks to me... he won't desire another woman, he will be fine only by my side, he will miss me and will come to meet me and ask me to never let him go... He will not eat, sleep or do anything unless he is with me, I trust the power of the Seven Crossroads and will continue spreading this powerful prayer, like this it is, it will be. ("The Forum Dedicated to Enochian and Magical Evocation")

On the other hand, the "Oración del puro" to Santa Muerte states:

> Soul of the four winds,
> you that go around the world,
> I want you to bring me so-and-so...
> by the seven spirits and the seven souls,
> make him change his love and come back to me,
> with the great power of Death.
> You that go around the world
> in streets, hills, neighborhoods,
> if you find so-and-so's soul...
> don't let him pass,
> until he comes exhausted to my feet;
> if he is sitting, don't let him be tranquil;
> put my thought in his mind;
> if he is sleeping make him dream about me,
> he will not be able to sleep calmly,
> as he will hear a child crying.
>
> (*Los poderes mágicos de la Santa Muerte* 20)

Both prayers appear to have antecedents in medieval magic. It is enough to recall the Maria Padilha *ponto cantado* discussed in chapter 3, in which "She lives in the gold mine/Where the black cock sings/Where the child does not cry" (Augras, "María Padilla" 301), or the song for Pombagira do Cruzeiro ("Pombagira of the Cross"):

> Your velvet cloak
> All embroidered with gold,
> Your fork is made of silver,
> Your treasure is very great!
>
> (Teixeira, *Enchantments* 23)

As is characteristic for liminal deities, Pombagira, similar to Baba Yaga and Kālī, appears identified here with the chthonic goddess that lives in the womb of the earth guarding her treasures of gold and silver; she is also both the goddess of death and the underworld and of fertility, symbolized by the black cock; and the lack of children crying may signify that this is not the realm of life but of death.

Pombagira and Santa Muerte developed in a hybrid cultural milieu, in which the population was Christianized by the Catholic Church, but where nevertheless remnants of preexisting religions are still very noticeable. In both African-based and in indigenous syncretism, Catholic saints and symbols were superimposed over their gods during colonial times. Nevertheless, while Afro-Latin American blending is usually visible and devotees tend to be conscious of it, Indo-Catholic syncretism is more camouflaged, as in the case of the Virgin of Guadalupe.[37] In addition, both Pombagira and Santa Muerte are polymorphous and in constant flux, which adds to their ambiguity. As noted earlier, they dwell in transition places, such as the streets, the crossroads, the cemetery, and their connection with death, as well as with love and sexuality, is strong. Although one of them is an incarnated spirit, usually embodied in a beautiful woman, and the other is an emaciated skeleton, they use similar colors and attributes, such as red and black, and offerings, such as candles, red flowers, cigarettes, and alcohol. As other beings that embody marginality and inferiority, they are both endowed with magical powers. They are believed to be extremely powerful and efficacious, and following the logic of market economy, they work for good or for evil for a price. Both are polysemic, ambivalent, postmodern deities, unfinished and in constant creation, similar to their impoverished and transient devotees, many of whom hold an ambiguous status within society. They also have their Catholic or semi-Catholic counterparts, such as Sara Kali and the Virgin Aparecida for Pombagira in Brazil and the Virgin of Guadalupe for Santa Muerte in Mexico. A softening agent in both cases is the influence of the goddess Iemanjá/Yemayá—a whitened image derived from Brazilian Umbanda—which today has been accepted as a national and even international icon of a young, white, ethereal woman with long black hair and a flowing blue gown, to whom collective, "national" rites are performed in Brazil (see figure 3.8), and it also exists as publicly displayed statues in Cuba. Nevertheless, this image is in itself a smoothed out representation of the black Yoruban goddess Yemoja that continues to persist in Brazilian Candomblé as Iemanjá and in Cuban Regla de Ocha as Yemayá.

Conclusion

A number of commonalities link the demonized fierce divinities of this book. Two of the most prominent characteristics of Baba Yaga, Kālī, Pombagira, and Santa Muerte are fragmentation and proximity to death. Pombagira's favorite dwelling place is the cemetery, and several of her avatars, such as Pombagira da Calunga, das Sete Calungas, da Sepultura, das Sete Sepulturas Rasas, and do Cemíterio, are explicitly linked to graveyards. Kālī lives on cremation grounds, eats flesh, and drinks blood, sometimes is depicted as emaciated and is adorned by body parts. Santa Muerte, portrayed as a skeleton, is death, and Baba Yaga is also the mistress of death, as she is instrumental in death rituals, has a "bony leg," a helper called Koshchey Bezsmertnyi ("Bony the Deathless"), and a home built of body parts. Fragmentation reduces them to substance and universal nature. Standing on the threshold of life and death, they are all mediators between worlds. In fact, these deities that at first sight seem so very different, most likely have a common origin in the Great Mother of the universe, who has cosmic control of existence—dominion over life, death, regeneration, and the transmutation of mater.[1]

These ambiguous and paradoxical figures embody the seeming opposites of life and teach us to look beyond them. All four are connected to death but also to sexuality and procreation, albeit in symbolic ways. For example, Baba Yaga's attributes—the mortar and the pestle—suggest the stirring of sexuality, and she often helps young couples to meet and procreate, as in the tale "Vasilisa prekrasnaia" ("Vasilisa the Fair"), discussed in chapter 1. Kālī is commonly portrayed in intercourse with her consort, Śiva, and during the Durgā Pūjā, Kālī's alter ego's festival, fertility is clearly celebrated through the *navapattrika*, the offering of bundles of nine different plants, various waters, as well as soils associated with fertility, such as earth dug with the tusk of a boar, a bull, or an elephant, and mud from the doors of prostitutes.[2] Pombagira, as prototype of a sacred harlot, is in charge of stirring the sexuality and fertility of the world, and Santa Muerte is also traditionally invoked for love and sexual magic.

Both Baba Yaga and Kālī, as well as Pombagira and Santa Muerte, are feminine divinities connected to liminality and the outskirts of civilization. Baba Yaga lives in a hut in a dense forest outside of a village and is linked to the Kalinovyi bridge on a river of fire that symbolizes a boundary between worlds. Kālī most likely originated among non-Arian, indigenous cultures that lived on the periphery of Indian society,[3] and today she is most popular among lower classes and women, and Pombagira's origin is in Bantu Africa as well as among the populace of medieval Europe. As Pombagira and Santa Muerte, Kālī is no stranger to crime and was the patron of the Thugs, combatted by the authorities as a band of thieves and murderers (Humes 155–61; Kinsley *Sword* 82). Interestingly, the geographic locations of these deities in today's world mimic their marginality, as they exist on the periphery of the "First World"—in Latin America, Slavic Eurasia, and India. Wildness and uncontrolled rage are also characteristics of Kālī and Pombagira. In addition, Pombagira and Santa Muerte are worshipped mainly by the excluded population of Brazil and Mexico, respectively, Santa Muerte being linked to illegal drug trafficking. Kālī, Pombagira, and Santa Muerte are connected to pragmatic results, and Baba Yaga fulfills this role symbolically in fairy tales as well. These four figures represent "the other," the dangerous, the uncontrollable and the uncomfortable, the forbidden, and the terrible; in sum—disorder—and a reversal of accepted ways imposed by dominant sectors of their respective societies.

Moreover, Pombagira and Santa Muerte are especially related, as they originated among similar Latin American, postcolonial conditions of extreme precariousness, poverty, marginalization, and insecurity of millions of people. For centuries, these individuals were subject to forced evangelization by the Catholic Church that condemns promiscuity, prostitution, crime, alcohol, smoking, and gambling—"the daily bread" of great sectors of subaltern classes surviving in provisional conditions. As a consequence, they often feel abandoned and excluded from official structure rights and develop an informal economy that also involves a parallel, self-generated symbolic and religious market. Similarly, their new devotions often become demonized and go "underground." Nevertheless, in spite of their marginalization, the unofficial deities empower and create a space for their worshippers, as they have a reputation of "getting things done." They help to revert the structure of power, giving strength to voiceless groups of population. They also expand beyond their original neighborhoods and cross borders, having an impact on many social and official circuits, such as TV shows, the press, art, film, and literature. They influence the collective imagination of entire nations, not only of the milieus that gave them life.

In spite of the fact that the four divine figures discussed in this book have been demonized or are depicted in diabolical ways, they are often preferred above "official" saints, such as the Virgin of Guadalupe, because the latter require following a strict moral code, and the former are seen as more powerful—"morally neutral," and all-accepting; they don't judge their devotees, and they admit people from all walks of life. In addition, they have been prominently featured in women's domestic worship. They also make us look beyond conformity and appearances. They are said to be dangerous, blood-thirsty, and may require blood sacrifices because they embody the ultimate truth of the universe that all matter is in constant change and has to be transmuted, ending in periodic destruction and death. Even though they have been rejected and maligned, they are most attractive to their devotees, as they represent the overcoming of opposites, wisdom, and magical powers, and therefore they are invoked for protection and strength.

There has been a long history of demonization of women on various continents, since ancient times. Examples are Lilith and her fall from the Canaanite Baalat or "Divine Lady" title to a sort of sexual demon whose daughters, the Lilim, "lustful she-demons," were succeeded by the Greek Empusae, "greedily seductive female demons," the Lamiae, and the succubae, the Christian "harlots of hell." They were all experts in lovemaking and asserted their sexual desires.[4] A continuation of this view of women can be seen since the Middle Ages in European persecutions of witches, women who were independent, practiced healing, midwifery, and often sorcery and sexual magic. In Western Europe, women were systematically tortured and executed under guidelines such as the fifteenth-century manual *Malleus Maleficarum (The Hammer of Witches)*, first published in Cologne, Germany, in 1487, which was used by inquisitors and judges to condemn them. Among the accusations was "female sexuality, seen as a powerful demonic force."[5]

Although Baba Yaga, Kālī Pombagira, and Santa Muerte originated in different parts of the world—Eastern Europe, India, Brazil, and Mexico—and their current portrayals are very diverse, they are reminiscent of the goddess of life, death, and regeneration, Queen of the Universe, that encompasses the life cycle, especially the aspects of this cycle omitted in current official devotions, such as death and putrefaction of the body, rage, fury, destruction, and sexuality. Despite the fact that they have been judged as evil or demonic, they are not constituted in terms of binary opposites, such as good and evil, but encompass the whole of life experience. Therefore, these unofficial holy figures[6] are closely linked to the Asian and American female shamans substituted by males, as well as to the persecuted European and African witches. Moreover, in contemporary Latin America, devotions to Pombagira and Santa Muerte reflect the uncertain circumstances of millions of subaltern and transient individuals that strongly identify with liminal divinities. Although the devotion to Kālī in India is very widespread, especially in West

Bengal, she is most revered by individuals who are excluded, voiceless, and living on the fringes of society. In addition, the devotion to Kālī in Trinidad and Guyana has many similarities with that of Pombagira in Brazil. Baba Yaga, on the other hand, was totally disallowed from any possible remnants of devotion and is currently used as a grotesque folkloric figure to laugh at and to scare children.

It is interesting to note that many popular worship personae that are the most ancestral and contain traits such as anger, sexuality, and an explicit connection to blood, death, and the periphery have been domesticated in different cultures, in an attempt to incorporate them in the dominant system of values and beliefs. Some examples are the orixá Iemanjá in Brazil, the unofficial saint Santa Muerte in Mexico, the witch Baba Yaga in Slavic Europe, and even the goddess Kālī in India. This may be due to social pressure to conform to "civilized" forces, usually forces of control imposed by the power hierarchy.

Because of their inferior status, polyvalence, ambiguity, independence, of being the representation of the rejected, the undesirable, and the forbidden, these untamed divinities equipped with supernatural powers are able to transcend the accepted aspects of society and to confront the devotee with the ultimate reality—that of chaos, impermanence, and death. Their frightening aspects and behaviors threaten the stability and order of society and put us face to face with primordial unpredictability and wildness—the hidden dimensions of reality. They teach us many uncomfortable lessons about human existence and can be very empowering. Consequently, they are often rejected and fought against by official institutions and by large sectors of the population. Like independent and fierce women healers and seers who did not conform to the established patriarchal order in the past, and as a consequence were persecuted and punished with banishment or death, today these fierce feminine divinities are often subjected to censorship through dismissal, demonization, dulcification, ridicule, or relegation to children's games and tales. Although these uncomfortable figures have been so marginalized, they have been able to transform and adapt, and they continue to be extremely attractive and powerful, reflecting the great need as well as the extraordinary resilience, resourcefulness, creativity, and ability of survival of their devotees.

Notes

Introduction

1. Victor Turner lists these three aspects of culture as "exceptionally well endowed with ritual symbols and beliefs of non-structural type" (*Dramas* 231).
2. Coatlicue ("Lady of the Serpent Skirt") is an Aztec Mother Goddess associated with death.
3. According to Turner, an example of the institutionalization of liminality may be found in the monastic and mendicant states in various world religions (*The Ritual* 107).
4. Walker, *Encyclopedia* 1077.
5. All translations from Spanish, Portuguese, French, Catalan, Polish, Russian, and Latin in this book are by the author, unless otherwise indicated.
6. For further discussion on this issue, see Sarlo 32–33 and Franco 223.
7. For a discussion of the sweetening of Kālī, see chapter 2 of this book.
8. Erndl, "The Play of the Mother" 152, among others.
9. I use the word "cult" to mean "devotion," in the same way that *culto* is used in Spanish.
10. In spite of the great similarities among these divinities, there is no cross-cultural book in English or in any other language that discusses and compares Baba Yaga, Kālī, Pombagira, and Santa Muerte in the United States or in any other country. In fact, there is not even a work that links any two of them. While there are studies that discuss the Hindu goddess Kālī, such as *Encountering Kālī* by McDermott and Kripal, eds., *Oh Terrifying Mother* by Sarah Caldwell, and *Kali* by Elizabeth U. Harding, one book on Baba Yaga (*Baba Yaga* by Andreas Johns), one on Pombagira (*Holy Harlots* by Kelly Hayes), and one on Santa Muerte (*Devoted to Death* by Andrew Chesnut), they focus exclusively on the Indian subcontinent, Russia, Brazil, and Mexico, respectively.

1 BABA YAGA, THE WITCH FROM SLAVIC FAIRY TALES

1. Among these scholars are Vladimir Propp and V. N. Toporov.
2. Propp identified seven main functions or roles in the magical Russian tales: the aggressor, the donor, the auxiliary, the princess and her father, the leader, the hero, and the false hero (*Morfología* 91).
3. For example, in the tale "Tsarevich Ivan and the Grey Wolf": "The Grey Wolf sprinkled the dead water on Tsarevich Ivan's wounds, and the wounds healed. Then he sprinkled him with Living water and Tsarevich Ivan came back to life" (Alexander 178). The healed wounds died, and the man became alive. Similarly, in the tales "Maria Morevna" and "The Flying Ship and the Marvelous Shirt," wounded or dismembered beings become whole and then alive by being sprinkled first with Dead Water and later with Live Water (*Baśnie* 73, 93, and 140). The Waters of Death serve to clean the dead from earthly elements in the Other World (Szyjewski 78).
4. (Hubbs 44). Although the turning spindle and the moon phases clearly belong to the feminine realm, they may be an example of later transformations of the tale, as suggested by Propp in "Las transformaciones de los cuentos maravillosos" (164–74).
5. Szafrański 64, 87, 145, following S. Poniatowski, *Etnografia Polski*, Warsaw: Wiedza o Polsce, vol. 3, n.d.: 261, 300.
6. The Hittites occupied the region of Anatolia (today's Turkey) in the second millennium BC.
7. In many ancient cultures dolls were considered receptacles of the souls of the dead. They were seated at the table, fed, and put to sleep. In fairy tales, they can be considered a borderline stage between guardian spirits and enchanted objects (Raíces 290–91). For example, in "Vasilisa the Fair," the doll represents the defunct mother of the girl. In Poland, *lale* (pl. of *lala*—"doll") were the wooden representations of the spirits of the dead. With time, *lale* or *lalki* were desemanticized, and today they mean "children's dolls" (Szyjewski 200). In Guatemala, it is customary to keep tiny dolls, *penitas* ("little worries"), and tell them one's *penas* or problems. In ancient Egypt and Peru (Tawantinsuyu), among other cultures, there was a cult of the mummies—the "doubles" of the dead—and in Peru, there were specially designated persons called *wauje* ("brothers") who enacted their movements during street processions.
8. For a discussion of the meaning of *korowody*, see Kohli 77, 156, and Oleszkiewicz-Peralba, *Black Madonna* 2 5, 29.
9. Taleinc ludedi nW osien183–86.
10. "The Firebird and Vasilissa-Tsarevna" (Wosien 183–86). Other formulas include: "Once upon a time, in a certain tsardom, in a

certain land" ("The Three Tsardoms, Copper, Silver and Golden," included in Wosien 171–82).
11. Tale #129, vol. 1, Afanasiev's collection, included in Wosien 171–82. Similarly, in Polish tales, the formula used is, "Ja też tam byłem, miód i wino piłem" ("I too was there and drank mead and wine").
12. V. Propp, *Russkaia Skazka*. Leningrad: Izdatel'stvo Leningradskovo Universiteta, 1984, 33–34, qtd. in Johns 48.
13. In different Slavic countries and regions, she exists under slightly different names, such as: Baba Jaga, Baba Jędza (Poland), Iezhibaba, Indzhibaba (Slovakia), Babaroga (Serbia), as well as Iagaia, Iagaba, Egibaba, Egibitsa, Egi-boba, Iagishna, Iagaia-Babitsa, Iaga, Babushka Liaga, Egishna, Indzhi-baba, among others, in Russia, Ukraine, and Byelarus (Johns 8).
14. "About the Girl Masha," tale recorded in 1939 from E. A. Vasil'eva in Korelia, included in Johns 291–94.
15. Boris Uspienskij, *Filologicheskije razyskanija v oblasti slavianskich drevnostej* (1982), qtd. in Szyjewski 128.
16. See Marija Gimbutas, *Goddesses and Gods* 135–37 and 144–45. According to Gimbutas, Old Europe was an autochthonous civilization dating from 7,000 to 3,500 BC, which encompassed mainly South-Central Europe (*Goddesses and Gods*16).
17. This is also true for the goddess Dhūmāvatī, discussed in chapter 2.
18. Tale "Stepmother and Stepdaughter," told by Anastasiia Gregorev'na Sotnikova and recorded in 1968 in the Niukhcha village of the Korelian coast, included in Johns 284–89.
19. With the advent of Christianity, the guardianship of cities was transferred to the God Birth-Giver, the Virgin Mary. An example is Our Lady of Ostra Brama (Matka Boska Ostrobramska), who still guards the gates of Vilnius, Lithuania, and people kneel to her in the middle of the street (my fieldwork, Vilnius, Lithuania, 1997).
20. This view was confirmed by my father, Eligiusz Oleszkiewicz, born and raised in Wilno (currently, Vilnius, capital of Lithuania).
21. Similarly, the *yaxche* or *ceiba*, sacred silk-cotton Tree of Life of the Mayans (kapok tree), venerated as *iroko* in Afro-Brazilian religions, and as *mapou* in Haiti, produces fruits full of cotton-like substance.
22. It is interesting to note that the Spinosaurus, the largest known predator who lived on earth 95 million years ago, had a head of a crocodile and a long neck and feet like a bird; the creature spent most of its time in water ("Spinosaurus Was Part Duck Part Crocodile," *Journal*, Link TV, September 12, 2014).
23. Nevertheless, there are still instances where Catholic saints are represented holding dragons, such as the statue of Saint Margaret in the church at Patzig, Germany (see Kohli, cover).

24. The Mothers, Àwọn Ìyàmi Òṣòròngà, represent the Àjẹ́ collective of the "Great and Mysterious Mothers." For a detailed discussion, see chapter 3 of this book, and Washington 1–70; the "Ìtàn-Oríkì" is qtd. in Washington 21.
25. For a detailed classification of colors, see Turner, *The Forest of Symbols* 5 9–111.
26. Swami Nikhilinananda, trans. *Upanishads*. New York: Harper & Row, 1963, qtd. in Turner, *Forest* 84–85.
27. Turner, *Forest* 85, following R. C. Zaehner, *Hinduism*. London: Oxford University Press, 1962: 91.
28. I am grateful to Dr. Yanko A. Yankov for gifting me with a selection of Bulgarian Martenitsas.
29. The frog, who undergoes a clear transformation during her life cycle, was a regenerative symbol of the goddess (Gimbutas, *Living Goddesses* 26). It was a fertility symbol related to Isis, Hecate, Hera, and Artemis (Kopaliński 503).
30. Aleksandr Potebnja, "O mificheskom znacheniinekotorykh obriadov I poverii. II. Baba Yaga." *Chteniia v imperatorskom obshchestvie istorii I drevnostei rossiiskikh pri moskovskom universitete* 1865 (3): 85–232, qtd. in Shapiro 121–22.
31. Propp reports that in original myths the hut was an animal or had zoomorphic traits (*Raíces* 83).
32. "Ivan Bykovich, the Cow's Son" and "The Frog-Tsarevna," included in Wosien 161 and 194 respectively.
33. V. F. Shevchenko, "Novye materialy po narodnoi pediatrii: 'sukhaia sten' I 'sobach'ia starost.'" In *Traditsionnaia kul'tura i mir detstva. Traditional Culture and the World of Childhood*. Ed. M. P. Cherednikova and V. F. Shevchenko. Ul'yanovsk: Laboratoriia kul'turologii, 1998: 112–20, qtd. in Johns 255.
34. My fieldwork, Salvador, Bahia, Brazil, 1996.
35. See Walker, *Encyclopedia* 819–21.
36. Interestingly, in Afro-Brazilian religions, especially in the most traditional Candomblé houses in Salvador, Bahia, these priestly functions are performed exclusively by women (*iyalorixás*), who form a kind of matriarchate. In less orthodox religious communities, there are male priests (*babalorixás*) as well, who nevertheless dress in women-like clothing and are frequently effeminate. In addition, the African male function of the *babalawo* was lost in Brazil. Another example of a culture where female shamans persist is the matrilocal and matrilineal Garífuna from northern Honduras. For Candomblé, see my book *The Black Black Madonna* 81–124; for the Garífuna, see Brondo 272–386 and Meza 250–77; and for other matriarchal societies around the world, see Goettner-Abendroth.

37. Following Heide Goettner-Abendroth, I use the term "matriarchy" to signify a gender-egalitarian society that emphasizes maternal values and symbols, where women are at the center. It is not equivalent to "patriarchy," but rather to "non-patriarchy" where power is shared.
38. In matrilocal societies, upon marriage, men join the wives' family homes.
39. In a matrilineal social structure, descent and inheritance are traced through the female line (Gimbutas, *Living*2 32).
40. An example is the story told about Fryderyk Chopin, who allegedly took a piece of "Mother Earth" with him when living Poland in1830.
41. *Povest' vremennykh let. Chast pervaya.* D. S. Likhachev, ed. and intro., Moskov/Leningrad: Izd. Ak. Nauk SSSR, 1950: 46, qtd. inKr avchenko 11.

2 Kālī, the Ultimate Fierce Feminine

1. Śakti—feminine energy (*śakti*), embodied as a goddess; *śākta*—pertaining to *śakti* (Kinsley, *Tantric* 285; Nagaswamy 1, 11–12).
2. Kinsley, *Tantric* 76, 90; Avalon xix–xxix. This chapter is based on primary materials, such as *The Bhāgavata Purāṇa*, *Mahānirvāna Tantra*, *Devī-māhātmyam*, *Karpūrādi-stotra*, *Grace and Mercy in Her Wild Hair* by Sen, and *Rama Prasada's Devotional Songs* by Sinha, as well as critical texts. In my discussion of the Ten Mahāvidyās, I am indebted to David Kinsey, *Tantric Visions of the Divine Feminine*.
3. Dr. Gayatri Devi first pointed out this connection to me in 2014.
4. For a discussion of the domestication of Kālī, see Gupta, "The Domestication of a Goddess."
5. Pombagira is considered an entity (*entidade*) rather than a goddess (*orixá*), as she embodies spirits from the past, but in practice her functions are those of a powerful goddess. A woman can be chosen and empowered in similar ways by a goddess or god (*orixá*) in the Brazilian religion Candomblé, but in this context advice giving is not performed during public ritual trances; instead, it is done during private consultations with the priestess (*iyalorixá*), usually through the sixteen-cowry divination system.
6. For case studies of women priestesses' empowerment through serving the Devī in India, see Erndl, "The Goddess and Women's Power" and "The Play of the Mother"; and for Pombagira in Brazil, see Hayes, *Holy Harlots* and "The Dark Side of the Feminine: Pomba Gira Spirits in Brazil."
7. For a discussion on Kālī worship in Trinidad, see McNeal, "Doing the Mother's Caribbean Work," and Caldwell, "Margins at Center."

For a discussion on Sara-La-Kâli worship by the Roma, see my article titled "Sara-La-Kâli: The Romani Black Black Madonna."
8. In this discussion of Kali Mai Puja, I follow Case, "The Intersemiotics of Obeah and Kali Mai in Guyana."
9. According to Frederick Ivor Case, in Kali Mai, the coconut represents Kālī, as they are both dark outside and light on the inside. In Guyanese as well as in other Afro-Latin American religious practices, the coconut, which has culinary as well as medicinal properties, acquired sacred value and may be used as an offering, in divination, and in the preparation of sacred foods, among others. In Afro-Cuban and Afro-Brazilian religions, the image of the trickster god Elleguá/Exu is usually made out of a coconut shell incrusted with cowry shells as eyes, nose, and mouth (see figure 3.9).
10. For further discussion, see Kohli 190, and Michaels et al., "Introduction" 16.

3 Pombagira, the Holy Streetwalker

1. "Com meu vestido vermelho/Eu venho p'ra girá!/Com meu colhar, brinco e pulseira,/Venho p'ra trabalhar!/Usodos melhores perfumes,/Para todos agradar,/Eu sou a Pomba-Gira, E vamos trabalhar!" (Bittencourt, "Pomba-Gira no seu vestido vermelho" 110).
2. Holy harlots or sacred prostitutes, also called "virgins" (from the Latin *virginem*, *virgo*—"maiden"), because they were unmarried priestesses, were common throughout the ancient world. For example, Ishtar, the Mother of Harlots, was called the Great Goddess and her high priestess, the Harine, was the spiritual ruler. The root of the word, signifying "strength" and "skill," was later applied to men, as in "virile." For a detailed discussion on this topic, see Briffault 3: 169; Sjöö; Walker, *Encyclopedia* 819–20; and *Assyrian and Babylonian* 170. For a discussion on parthenogenesis, see *Virgin Mother Goddesses of Antiquity* and *The Cult of Divine Birth in Ancient Greece* by R igoglioso.
3. In reality, rather than "gods," *orixás* "are the varied and multifaceted manifestations of all the divine energies in the universe that together would constitute God." Therefore, it is erroneous to describe Afro-Latin American religions as polytheistic (West-Durán 296).
4. SeeS heilaW alker," Candomblé"12.
5. The first African slave groups brought to Brazil beginning 1516 through the sixteenth, seventeenth, and the first half of the eighteenth century were predominantly from the Bantu culture, corresponding to today's Congo-Angola region. By mid-eighteenth century through the end of slavery in Brazil in 1888, a great concentration of Yoruba slaves, from the area of today's Nigeria and

Benin, were brought to Brazil, greatly influencing the local culture and creating syncretic religions, such as Candomblé.
6. Santa Sara Kali or Kali Sara is a Brazilian version of Sara-La-Kâli, worshipped at Les Saintes-Maries-de-la-Mer in southeastern France, during an enormous yearly Roma pilgrimage and festival that includes processions to the sea, resembling the Indian Durgā Pūjā, and Catholic masses. Although Sara-La-Kâli is not an official saint, at Les Saintes-Maries, she has been incorporated into Catholic celebrations, together with the Saint Maries—Marie Jacobé and Marie Salomé—who allegedly arrived to Camargue in AD 42 together with Mary Magdalene, escaping persecutions in Palestine. In the process, Mary Magdalene—the most important passenger of the boat—has been eliminated from the trinity of Maries. For further discussion on this topic, see my article titled "Sara-La-Kâli: The Romani Black Black Madonna."
7. Umbanda—a highly syncretic Brazilian religion discussed further in this chapter. Quimbanda—stigmatized as a backward religion that deals with black magic. In practice, both seem to be intrinsically linked and one hardly exists without the other.
8. Obatalá is syncretized with Virgen de las Mercedes (Virgin of Mercy) in Cuba and with Jesus Christ in Brazil (as Oxalá), which suggests that this powerful *orisa* (*orixá*) encompasses both feminine and masculine qualities.
9. Pontos cantados ("sacred songs") and *pontos riscados* ("sacred drawings") serve to invoke Exus and Pombagiras in Umbanda/Quimbanda.
10. "Inhansã, que lhe deu força/E Rainha no Candomblé,/Vamos saravá a Rainha/ Pomba Gira Exu Mulher" (Molina 97; translation Eva Bueno).
11. For further discussion, see Prandi, "Pombagiras" 92, and Brumana and Martinez 188. Similarly, Santa Muerte is often addressed as *señora*.
12. "Ela é mulher de sete maridos,/Não mexa com ela,/Pombagira é perigo" (Capone, *A busca*111).
13. "Pombagira é amansador/De burro brabo/Amansai o meu marido/Com seiscientos mil diabos" (ibid., 112).
14. "Meu Santo Antônio pequenino/Amansador de touro bravo/Quem mexer com Maria Padilha/Está mexendo com o diabo" (Augras," MaríaP adilla"314) .
15. "Pomba-Gira e seu destino/O meu destino é este:/É me divertir!/ Bebo, fumo, pulo e danço,/Para subsistir!/Assim cumpro o meu destino,/Que é só me divertir!" (Bittencourt, "Pomba-Gira no seu vestido vermelho" 110).
16. Axel Michaels et al., eds., *Wild Goddesses* 10, 15; Harle 245; Samanta, among others.

17. For a discussion of colors, see chapter 1 and the specific section in this chapter; for Kālī,s ee chapter 2.
18. Similarly, in Christianity, the two extremes are represented by the Virgin Mary and Eve.
19. *Karpūrādi-stotra*, "Prayer"; *Devī-māhātmyam* Ch. 11:11; Rishi, *Roma* 78; McDaniel, *Offering Flowers* 243–44.
20. Augras," MariaP adilha" 301.
21. For further discussion on this topic, see Marija Gimbutas, "Women and Culture in Goddess-Oriented Old Europe" 23.
22. This is a frequent motif in Baba Yaga's tales.
23. Allan Kardec (Léon Hyppolyte Dénizart Rivail), 1804–1869, was a French science teacher who systematized Spiritism as a blend of religion, science, and philosophy. His most famous work is *The Books of Spirits*, first published in 1857 in France and in 1875 in Brazil. Kardec's teachings became very popular among Brazilian bourgeoisie who wanted to distance themselves from African worship. The Umbanda religion was created by reintegrating ancient African elements, among others, into Kardecism.
24. Marcelo was initiated in the Candomblé religion in 1978 and established the Tzara Ramirez in 1992, named after Anrez Ramirez, the Gypsy spirit he incorporates. He was trained as a *babalao* to read the Yoruba Ifá oracle in Candomblé; at Tzara Ramirez, he conducts prayers, baptisms, card readings, and healings (Vidal).
25. *Roça*—Afro-Brazilian religious community, literally "countryside."
26. See the article "O caso da Pombagira. Religião e violencia: uma análise do jogo discursivo entre umbanda e sociedade" by Contins andGoldma n.
27. The history of the Roma in Brazil goes back to colonial times, when part of the ethnic and religious persecutions in Portugal, which generally involved the galley for men, was changed to deportation to the colony in the case of João de Torres and his family, in 1574. This event established Brazil as the first country on the American continent that received Gypsies. However, the practice of their exile was not generalized until 1686. Most of the circa one million Roma inhabiting Brazil today are of Iberian, Caló descent, and many of them are incorporated into the mainstream of the population. They first arrived from Western Europe to Spain in the mid-fifteenth century and from there to Portugal at the end of the fifteenth or the beginning of the sixteenth century (China 57–59). In fact, according to Perly Cipriano, subsecretary for the Promotion and Defense of Human Rights of the Special Secretariat for Human Rights of the Republic's Presidency, SEHD, Brazil has the second largest Gypsy population in the world ("Projeto Cidadania de Ciganos e Nômades e Lancado na

ALMG"). In addition, one of the most successful presidents, who established Brazil's economic development and funded the new capital, Brasilia, was Juscelino Kubitschek (1956–1961), who publicly suggested his Roma descent in 1960. This presence influenced the culture of Brazil, where the Roma people were appropriated and symbolically accommodated. In the past 20 years, there have been a number of developments regarding the Roma. In 1987, the Center of Gypsy Studies (CEC) in Brazil was formed, and the first Week of Gypsy Culture in Latin America was celebrated (Costa, *Os ciganos* 10). One of the most notable events of recent years was the establishment of the National Day of the Gypsy People by President Luiz Inácio Lula da Silva on May 25, 2006. The Roma lawyer Miriam Stanescon Rorarni was instrumental in this development. Another evolution is the appearance in Brazil of a number of Gypsy *tzaras* or "tents," structured as healing centers that provide a number of services and rituals.

28. "De vermelho e negro/Vestida na noite o mistério traz/Ela é moça bonita/Oi, girando, girando, girando lá" (Prandi, "Pombagiras" 93).
29. Washington 28–29; Turner, *Forest* 107. For further discussion on red, white, and black color symbolism, see chapter 1 of this book.
30. Around four million immigrants entered Brazil between 1880 and 1930, with one million arriving between 1880 and 1890 (Martine and McGranahan 8). Rio de Janeiro's population tripled between 1890 and 1920.
31. For discussion of Santa Muerte, see chapter 4.
32. Because of colonization, a patriarchal shift occurred in Africa, where these mighty female deities and women started to be identified with evil forces and called "witches" (Washington 6).
33. "Possuidora de asas magníficas, minha mãe Òṣòròngà./Possuidora de asas magníficas, minha mãe Òṣòròngà./Eu a saúdo, não me mate minha mãe./Eu a saúdo, não me cause perturbações minha mãe./Se você vem perto de nós, oh proteja-nos!" (qtd. in Santos, *Os nàgô e a morte*193) .
34. Zé Pilintra, a very popular Exu figure, is allegedly based on a real-life character who lived in Recife, Brazil, in the 1930s.
35. SeeB urdick.
36. Augras, "María Padilla" 28. For Kardecism, see note #23.
37. "Sou Maria Padilha/Dos 7 Cruzeiros/Tenho força das Almas/Dos velhos do cativeiro/Trabalhamos unidos,/Numa só braçada,/Sou Maria Padilha/Formosa e muito amada" (Ribeiro 83).
38. *Cavalo*—horse, *burro*—donkey. Denominations given to people who enter into trances incorporating entities in the Candomblé and Umbanda religions, respectively. Nevertheless, the derogatory term *burro* is not used in the more Africanized types of Umbanda.

39. Reginaldo Prandi, in his 1994 article "Pombagiras dos Candomblés e Umbandas e as faces inconffessas do Brasil" (99), reports that ritual animal sacrifice has practically disappeared from Umbanda, but there are variations from *terreiro* to *terreiro*.
40. This classification is inspired by Capone, *Searching* 77.
41. During my 1996 stay in Salvador, Brazil, I was invited to only one Mesa Branca ("White Table") ceremony by the practitioners of the Candomblé Nagô *terreiro*, Ilê Asé Orisanlá J'Omin, because it was considered of a lower status than Candomblé. Nevertheless, often the same individuals are simultaneously involved in two or more religions (e.g., Candomblé, Spiritism, and Catholicism).
42. In the Galicia region of Spain, there was and still is a distinction between *meigas* and *bruxas*. *Meigas* are the "holy women" and "wise women," and *bruxas* are considered evil witches. The Galician *meiga* corresponds to the Spanish *maga* or *hechicera*—"a female magician." It can be said that "[s]anta and bruxa ('holy woman' and 'witch') are two aspects of the *meiga* concept and together express what has been very aptly called the awe of the inexplicable" (Rey-Henningsen 200–201).
43. Iroko—sacred tree with magical powers, venerated in Africa as well as in Afro-Brazilian *terreiros*; kind of kapok or ceiba tree.
44. Prakrti—Creatrix of nature, both with and without form (*Devī-māhātmyam*45).
45. For discussion on the transfer of power from female to male and on Ìyàmi Òṣòròngà, see Cunha 2–3, 6, 9; Capone, *Searching* 61; Augras, "De Iyá mi" 20; and Santos, *Os nàgô e a morte* 123.
46. For example, see the novel *Bless Me Última*, by Rudolfo Anaya.
47. According to Cros, "In the most ancient myths, Odùduwà appears as a creator goddess, prior to Obatalá himself, and contemporary to Olódùmaré. The goddess Odùduwà is the feminine principle, the fertile creator mother to whom pregnant women render homage. She is represented as a woman suckling her son and is considered mother of the Yoruba race" (141).
48. Washington 37–38, following interviews with Samuel M. Opeola; William Bascom, *Sixteen Cowries*; and Drewal and Drewal, Gẹlẹdẹ.
49. According to Augras, the first great public feast for Iemanjá took place at the Leme beach in Rio de Janeiro on the night of January 31, 1957 ("De Iyá mi" 29). Nevertheless, Iemanjá keeps her dark skin color as well as her tempestuous and demanding aspects in the practice of Brazilian Candomblé and the Cuban Regla de Ocha (as Yemayá).
50. IncludedinB eier11.
51. The practice of Umbanda and the worship of Pombagira spread to countries bordering with Brazil, such as Argentina, Uruguay, and Paraguay.

52. Currently, around 2.5 million people live in Rio's *favelas*, which constitutes over a third of the entire city's population (*Aquí y Ahora*,Uni visión,Ap ril6,2014) .
53. "Ele é dono da rua/com sua gira pesada/age em vários setores/ cemitérios e encruzilhada/por isso muitas vezes/sem Exu não se faz nada" (Meyer 103).

4 Santa Muerte, Death the Protector

1. "Muerte Querida de mi corazón, no me desampares de tu protección" (popular prayer to Santa Muerte).
2. "No sé si exista Dios, pero la muerte sí...La muerte es más fuerte que la vida, pues acaba con ella...Ante la falta del sentido de la vida, hay un exceso del sentido de la muerte." Testimonies of Santa Muerte devotees from Tepito, included in "Devoción a la Santa Muerte y San Judas Tadeo en Tepito y anexas" by Hernández.
3. A short version of this chapter was presented at the *Death & Dying Symposium* in Houston, Texas, on October 25, 2012, and published in the electronic *Proceedings* in November 2013, as well as in my article "Święta Śmierć, Nasza Opiekunka: Meksykańska Santa Muerte/Holy Death, Our Protectress: The Mexican Santa Muerte" (*Etnografia nowa/The New Ethnography* 5, 2013).
4. "Archbishop" David Romo Guillén, who was sentenced to 12 years in prison for electoral fraud in 2011, and to 66 years for extorsion and kidnapping in 2012 ("Dan 66 años"; "Líder de la iglesia"), was not accepted by the Catholic Church nor by many Santa Muerte worshippers. For further discussion on Santa Muerte and her imagery, see the DVD *La Santa Muerte* by Eva Aridjis and the book *Devoted to Death* by C hesnut.
5. For a detailed discussion of the goddess Iemanjá/Yemayá, see Chapter 3 of my book *The Black Madonna in Latin America and Europe*.
6. Sara-La-Kâli, a Virgin Mary–like statue placed in the subterranean crypt of the church at Les Saintes Maries-de-la Mer in southeastern France, is an unofficial patron saint and the object of veneration of the Roma who gather there by thousands for her annual May festival. For further discussion on this topic, see my article "Sara-La-Kâli: The Romani Black Madonna."
7. Some examples are Mi Niña Blanca ("My White Girl"), La Madrina ("The Godmother"), La Hermana Blanca ("The White Sister"), La Doña ("The Lady"), La Jefa ("The Boss"), La Santa Niña ("The Holy Girl"), La Señora ("The Lady"), La Señora Blanca ("The White Lady"), La Señora Negra ("The Dark Lady"), La Flaca ("The Skinny One"), La Flaquita ("The Little Skinny One"), La Huesuda ("The

Bony One"), La Calaca (familiar and humorous way in which death is referred to in Mexican culture), La Dama Poderosa ("The Powerful Lady"), La Comadre (name by which the mother of a child and his/her godmother call each other), Santísima Muerte ("Most holy Death"), La Santita ("The Little Saint"), Mi Rosa Maravillosa ("My Marvelous Rose"), La Hermana Blanca ("The White Sister"), and Mi Niña Guapa ("My good-looking Girl").
8. Materials include raisin, plaster, wood, stone, concrete, copper, silver, gold, platinum, as well as corn, wheat, and vegetables (Gil 103; Roush 131).
9. When in the early 2000s I mentioned to some of my Mexican students that I was finally ready to get married, I was quickly advised to place a Saint Anthony's statue upside down and leave it thus until he delivered me a husband. Needless to say, my wish was soon fulfilled.
10. The earlier section is based on Andrew Chesnut's, Eva Aridjis's, and my own fieldwork observations.
11. *Noticiero Nocturno*, Univisión, November 3, 2013; Gil 18, 13, 84.
12. *Curandero/a*—folk healer in the Native Latin American traditions; *Diloggún*—16-cowry divination system used in Santería; Palo Mayombe—an Afro-Cuban religion. Santero—devotee of the Afro-Cuban religion, Santería or Regla de Ocha.
13. For example, *Botánica Domínguez* and *Botánica Ven a Mí* do not carry Santa Muerte images or services.
14. Te ha[s] convertido en un ser muy especial en mi vida
    Tepi enso a cada instante y mi fe por ti a cada momento crece
    Desde que te conozco ya no me siento s[o]la
    Sé que Dios te mand[ó] a m[í] para que te pida con mucho amor
    T[ú] quieres lo mejor para tus hijos y sabes bien qu[é] hay en nuestros corazones
    Entonces mi niña ya conoces bien el mío
    Conoces todo de m[í], sabes todas mis necesidades y por eso con gran amor te pido
    En mi corazón te llevo por siempre.
    ("Agradecimientop arami N iñaB lanca")
15. For further information on this issue, see Gil 115–25.
16. For detailed discussion, see the "Historical Antecedents" section in this chapter.
17. *Noticiero Nocturno*,Uni visión,Oc tober20, 2012.
18. See quote by Thomassen in the Introduction.
19. Mónica Salazar, presentation at the *Art of Death & Dying Symposium*, University of Houston, Texas, October 25, 2012.
20. See interview with the artist in Nery 271–78, 233.
21. I mainly refer to Chicano/a artists in the United States, such as Yolanda M. López, Ester Hernandez, and Alma Lopez, who

modified and even reversed the meaning of the Mexican national icon. For more information, see Chapter 4 of my book *The Black Madonna in Latin America and Europe*.
22. La Llorona ("The Weeping Woman") is a Mexican mythical figure that represents a betrayed mother who weeps because of the loss of her children; she is a symbol frequently found in Mexican literature and folklore. Her role is transformed according to changing socialc ircumstances.
23. JohnM artin,p ersonali nterview.
24. Devotional books include: *La Biblia de la Santa Muerte*; *Práctica del culto a la Santa Muerte* by Guttman; *El libro de la Santa Muerte* by Velázquez; and *Los poderes mágicos de la Santa Muerte*, among others.
25. They include the "Prayer to Ask for Advice," "Prayer to Solve Family Problems," "Prayer to End a Family Conflict," "Prayer of Financial Difficulties," "Prayer for Abundance and Finances," "Prayer for Health of the Body," "Prayer to Take Away a Vice," "Prayer to Protect Children," "Prayer to Avoid Robbery," "Prayer to Take Care of Work," "Prayer for Business," "Prayer to Protect a Business," "Prayer to Cleanse a Business," "Incantation for Good Luck," "Prayer to Attract Good Fortune in Business and at Home," "Prayer to Attract a Loved Person," and "Prayer to Enjoy Protection during a Trip" (*La Biblia de la Santa Muerte*, 2010: 94).
26. In San Antonio, Texas, this cult is predominantly individual. No public ceremonies or events are performed, as devotees are afraid of stigmatization. Nevertheless, in several US cities, such as Los Angeles and San Diego, there exist public devotional centers.
27. An example of such a congregation is the Irmandade da Boa Morte or "Sisterhood of the Good Death" of Cachoeira, Bahia, Brazil; for further discussion, see my book *The Black Madonna in Latin America and Europe*.
28. For a discussion on this topic in regard to Kālī, see Vrinda Dalmiya, "Loving Paradoxes" 144.
29. This is exemplified in the works of such European painters as Albert Durer (1471–1528), Hans Holbein (1497–1543) and his *Dance of Death*, and Pieter Bruegel the Elder's (1525–1569) *Triumph of Dead*. A written example are the verses of the Spaniard Pedro López de Ayala (1332–1407):
 You well know, for sure, and ought not doubt,
 That death doesn't know how to pardon anyone,
 The big and the small, she will kill all,
 And all in common will experience her.
 (Kuersteiner vol. 2: 94, quadrant 553)

30. Perdigón 27–30; Gil 14. These death chariots, without the skeletal figure, continue to be used to this day, especially in funerals of important or famous individuals. At first, they were carriages or hearses pulled by horses, as, for example, in the funeral of King Louis XVIII's and of Abraham Lincoln; with the implementation of cars, they were replaced by luxurious and elaborate funerary vehicles.
31. San Pascual was a historical figure, born in the Aragón province of Spain in 1540. He joined the Franciscan order in 1565. Because of his exemplary life, after his death in 1592, he was beatified in 1618 and canonized in 1690. These occasions were celebrated by the Franciscan friars in Guatemala where this particular cult was born. For a detailed discussion on the figures that preceded Santa Muerte, see Malvido, "Crónicas" 24–25 and Navarrete 22–23, 34.
32. The Cihuateteo were Aztec women deified by death in childbirth.
33. For example, the Mayan culture, dating from the Classical Period (ca. 100 BC–AD 900), created a complex system of coordinated calendars—the sacred lunar calendar of 260 days, the solar calendar of 365 days, and the Venusian calendar of 584 days, which cyclicallyc oincided.
34. Acaso de verdad se vive en la tierra?
    No para siempre en la tierra: sólo un poco aquí.
    Aunque sea de jade se quiebra,
    aunque sea de oro se rompe,
    aunque sea plumaje de quetzal se desgarra,
    no para siempre en la tierra: sólo un poco aquí.
    (Thes ageN ezahualcóyotl,qtd.i nL eón-Portilla 122).
35. Sólo venimosa dor mir,
    sólov enimos a soñar:
    ¡No es verdad, no es verdad
    que venimos a vivir en la tierra!...
    Algunas flores produce nuestro cuerpo
    y por allá queda marchito. ("La vida es sueño," *Cantares Mexicanos*, pholio 14, line 3, qtd. in Garibay 60).
36. Death is also present in Mexican literature, from the eighteenth century (1792) novel by Joaquín Bolaños, *La portentosa vida de la muerte*, with a female Death as a main character, to such twentieth-century novels as the 1955 *Pedro Páramo* by Juan Rulfo, in which all the characters, including the narrator, are deceased, to the traditional Day of the Dead poems or *calaveras*, an extended list of films, such as *La muerte enamorada* (1950), *Macario* (1959), *El jinete de la muerte* (1981); on the ring as the *luchador enmascarado* ("masked fighter"), in folk burlesque proverbs and sayings

referring to death, such as *amaneció muerto* ("he/she woke up dead") *colgar los tenis* ("to hang the snickers"), *entregar el equipo* ("to return the equipment"), *al diablo la muerte mientras la vida nos dure* ("to the devil with death while life continues") (Perdigón 50–54), as well as in other expressions of popular culture, such as the Lotería ("lottery") cards. Currently, the figure of Santa Muerte also entered the Mexican everyday life and arts.

37. For a detailed discussion on this topic, see my book *The Black Madonna in Latin America and Europe*.

Conclusion

1. The word "mater," which means "mother" in Latin, has an obvious relation to "mother." The Divine Mother of the *Devī-māhātmyam* is the "origin of all the worlds," the "supreme, primordial Prakrti" ("Creatrix," "Nature") (*Devī-māhātmyam* Ch. 4: 7). The Christian Virgin Mary, called Mother of God and God's Birth-Giver, is also invoked by her devotees as a strong and protective mother. For a discussion on this topic, see my book *The Black Madonna in Latin America and Europe*.
2. Ghosha41– 51; *Mahānirvāna Tantra*328.
3. For a discussion of cultures living on the periphery of Indian society, see Kinsley, *Hindu Goddesses* 96, and *The Sword and the Flute* 85. For a discussion of the "Great" or "Indo-Aryan," "Brahmanic," "Vedic," or "orthodox" tradition, as well as the "little" or "Dravidian," "tribal," "indigenous," or "regional" tradition, see Kinsley, *The Sword and the Flute* 83. Nevertheless, since the earlier reflects the Brahmanic view represented by a minority, and Kālī is in fact worshipped by the majority of the Indian population, this view may be contested, as in Humes, "Wrestling with Kālī " (155–61).
4. For further discussion on this topic, see Graves and Patai, *Hebrew Myths* 68–69; Graves, *The Greek Myths* vol 1: 189–90 and 205–206; and Walker, *Encyclopedia*541–42.
5. Hoch-Smith 246–47. See the complete *Malleus Malleficarum* translations by Kramer and Sprenger (1928) and by Mackay (2009).
6. The Indian Kālī is the only one of them officially accepted as a goddess.

Bibliography

Abreu, Mauricio de A. *Evolução urbana de Rio de Janeiro*. 1987. Rio de Janeiro: Instituto Pereira Passos, 2006. Print.
Afanas'ev, Aleksandr. *Russian Fairy Tales*. 1945. Trans. Norbert Guterman; Illustr. Alexander Alexeieff; Comment, Roman Jocobson. New York: Pantheon, 1973. Print.
"Agradecimiento para mi Niña Blanca by Rocío." February 24, 2010. Web. October 22, 2012. http://nuestrasantamuerte.glogspot.com.
Alexander, Alex E., trans. *Russian Folklore: An Anthology in English Translation*. Belmont: Nordland, 1975. Print.
Anaya, Rudolfo. *Bless Me, Última*. 1972. New York: Warner Books, 1999. Print.
Aquí y Ahora. Univisión, Miami, April 6, 2014. Television.
Aridjis, Eva, dir. *La Santa Muerte*. Dark Night Pictures, 2007. DVD.
Aridjis, Homero. *La Santa Muerte: sexteto del amor, las mujeres, los perros y la muerte*. Mexico City: Alfaguara, 2003. Print.
Assyrian and Babylonian Literature: Selected Translations. New York: Appleton, 1901. Print.
Augras, Monique. "De Iyá mi a Pomba-Gira: transformações e símbolos da libido." Moura, *Candomblé* 17–44. Print.
———. "María Padilla, reina de la magia." *Revista Española de Antropología Americana* 31 (2001): 293–319. Print.
Avalon, Arthur. "Introduction." *Mahānirvāna Tantra* xvii–cxlvi. Print.
Bairrão, José Francisco Miguel Henriques. "Subterrâneos da submissão: sentidos do mal no imaginário umbandista." *Bairrão* (2002): 55–67. Web. September 2012. http://www.fafich.ufmg.br.
Barnstone, Willis, ed. *The Other Bible*. New York: HarperCollins, 1984. Print.
Barros, Cristiane Amaral de. "Iemanjá e Pomba-Gira: imagens do feminino na Umbranda." MS thesis. Universidade Federal de Juiz de Fora, 2006. Print.
Baśnie rosyjskie. Trans. Ewa Morycińska-Dzius. Warsaw, Poland: RYTM, 2013. Print.
Batalla, Juan, and Danny Barreto, eds. *Dueños de la encrucijada: estéticas de Exú y Pomba Gira en el Río de la Plata*. Buenos Aires: Arte Brujo, 2008. Print.

Bayley, Harold. *The Lost Language of Symbolism.* Vols 1 and 2, 1912. London: Bracken, 1996. 2 vols. Print.
Beier, Ulli. "Gelede Masks." *Odu* 6 (1958): 5–24. Print.
Bhabha, Homi K. *The Location of Culture.* London and New York: Routledge, 1994. Print.
The Bhāgavata Purāṇa. Trans. and annot. Ganesh Vasudeo Tagare. 1976. Delhi: Motilal Banarsidass, 1979. 3 Vols. Print.
La Biblia. Madrid and Estrella: San Pablo and Editorial Verbo Divino, 1995. Print.
La Biblia de la Santa Muerte. Mexico City: Editores Mexicanos Unidos, 2010. Print.
La Biblia de la Santa Muerte. Mexico: Ediciones S.M., n.d. Print.
Birman, Patricia. "Identidade social e homossexualismo no candomblé." *Religião e Sociedade* 12 (1985): 2–21. Print.
———. "Laços que nos unem: ritual, família e poder na umbanda." *Religião e Sociedade* 8 (1982): 21–27. Print.
———. "Transas e Transes: Sexo e gênero nos cultos afro-brasileiros, um sobrevoo." *Estudos Feministas* 13.2 (2005): 403–14. Print.
Birnbaum, Lucia Chiavola. *Dark Mother.* Lincoln: iUniverse, 2001. Print.
Bittencourt, José Maria. *No Reino dos Exus.* 6th ed. Rio de Janeiro: Pallas, 2006. Print.
Boas, Franz. *Indian Myths & Legends from the North Pacific Coast of America.* 1895. Ed. Randy Bouchard and Dorothy Kennedy; Trans. Dietrich Bertz. Vancouver: Talon Books, 2002. Print.
Bourdieu, Pierre. "Genesis and Structure of the Religious Field." *Comparative Social Research* 13 (1991): 1–44. Print.
Bourguignon, Erika. "Suffering and Healing Subordination and Power: Women and Possession Trance." *Ethos* 32.4 (2004): 558–74. Print.
Bowker, John. *World Religions.* New York: DK Publishing, 1997. Print.
Briffault, Robert. *The Mothers.* Vols 2 and 3. New York: Macmillan, 1927. 3 Vols. Print.
Brondo, Keri Vacanti. "La pérdida de la tierra y el activismo de las mujeres garífunas en la costa norte de Honduras." *Journal of International Women's Studies* 9.3 (2008): 372–94. Web. May 12, 2013. http://www.vc.bridgew.edu.
Brumana, Eduardo Giobellina, and Elda Gonzales Martínez. *Spirits from the Margin: Umbanda in Sao Paulo.* Uppsala: Acta Universitatis Upsaliensis. Uppsala: Almqvist, 1989. 2 Vols. Uppsala Studies in Cultural Anthropology 12. Print.
Burdick, John. "Gossip and Secrecy: Women's Articulation of Domestic Conflict in Three Religions of Urban Brazil." *Sociological Analysis* 50.2 (1990): 153–70. Print.

Caburn, Thomas B. "Devī: The Great Goddess." *Devī: Goddesses of India.* Eds. John S. Hawley and Donna M. Wulff. Berkeley: University of California Press, 1996. 31–48. Print.

"Calaquita de San Pascualito." *Falsaria.com.* Falsaria, June 11, 2012. Web. October 22, 2012. http://www.falsaria.com.

Caldwell, Sarah. "Margins at Center." McDermott, *Encountering Kālī* 247–72. Print.

———. *Oh Terrifying Mother: Sexuality, Violence and Worship of the Goddess Kāḷi.* New Delhi: Oxford University Press, 1999. Print.

———. "Worship of the Goddess in Hinduism." 25th Anniversary Conference of the Sri Venkateswara Temple in Pittsburgh, Pittsburgh 2000. Web. February 23, 2010. http://www.infinityfoundation.com.

Campbell, Joseph. *The Mythic Image.* Princeton: Princeton University Press, 1974. Print.

Capone, Stefania. *A busca da África no candomblé: tradição e poder no Brasil.* Trans. Procópio Abreu. Rio de Janeiro: Pallas, 2004. Print.

———. *Searching for Africa in Brazil: Power and Tradition in Candombé.* Trans. Lucy Lyall Grant. London: Duke University Press, 2010. Print.

Caroso, Carlos, and Jeferson Bacelar, eds. *Faces da tradição afro-brasileira: religiosidades, sincretismo, anti-sincretismo, reafricanização, práticas terapêuticas, etnobotánica e comida.* 2nd ed. Trans. Cristina Warth. Rio de Janeiro: Pallas, 1999. Print.

Carybé. *Iconografia dos deuses africanos no candomblé da Bahia.* Sao Pablo: Raízes, 1980. Print.

Case, Frederick Ivor. "The Intersemiotics of Obeah and Kali Mai in Guyana." *Nation Dance.* Ed. Patrick Taylor. Bloomington: Indiana University Press, 2001. 40–53. Print.

Castells Ballarin, Pilar. "La Santa Muerte y la cultura de los derechos humanos." *Liminar* 6.1 (2008): 13–25. February 19, 2008. *Redalyc.* Web. November 1, 2013.

Castiñeiras, Manuel. *El tapiz de la creación.* Girona, Spain: Catedral de Girona, 2011. Print.

Cervantes, Miguel de. *Los trabajos de Persiles y Sigismunda.* Ed. Florencio Sevilla Arroyo. Biblioteca Virtual Miguel de Cervantes, 2001. Web. July 6, 2006. http://www.cervantesvirtual.com.

Chesnut, R. Andrew. *Devoted to Death.* New York: Oxford University Press, 2012. Print.

China, J. B. d' Oliveira. *Os ciganos do Brasil.* Sao Paulo: Imprensa Oficial do Estado, 1936. Print.

Chitgopekar, Nilma, ed. *Invoking Goddesses: General Politics in Indian Religion.* New Delhi: Shaktibooks, 2002. Print.

"The Church of the Santa Muerte Fights Back." *Dream Act.* March 30, 2009. Web. October 22, 2012. http://dreamacttexas.blogspot.com.

Clarke, Peter B., ed. *New Trends and Developments in African Religions.* Greenwood Press: Westport, CT and London, 1998. Print.

The Complete Works of Sister Nivedita. Vols 1 and 2. Calcutta, India: Ramakrishna Sarada Mission Sister Nivedita Girls' School, 1967. 2 Vols. Print.

La Concha, Gerardo de. "La Santa Muerte." *Reforma.com.* Reforma, November 7, 2004. Web. October 18, 2011. http://galegroup.com.

Contins, Marcia, and Marcio Goldman. "O caso da Pombagira. Religião e violência: uma análise do jogo discursivo entre umbanda e sociedade." *Religião e sociedade* 11.1 (1985): 103–32. Print.

Cordova, Nery. *La narcocultura: simbología de la transgresión, el poder y la muerte.* Culiacán, Mexico: Universidad Autónoma de Sinaloa, 2011. Print.

Correa Cabrera, Guadalupe. "Violence in the 'Forgotten' Border: Unemployment, Edemic Corruption, and the Paramilitarization of Drug Cartels on the Texas-Tamaulipas Border." Symposium *Bridging Cultures.* San Antonio, November 9, 2012. Conference.

Correa, Pablo. "El culto a la Santa Muerte." *ElEspectador.com.* Especial para El Espectador México, October 18, 2011. Web. October 22, 2012. http://www.ElEspectador.com.

Costa, C. da. *Os ciganos continuam na estrada.* Rio de Janeiro: Libro Arte, 1989. Print.

Cros Sandoval, Mercedes. *La religión afrocubana.* Madrid, Spain: Playor, 1975. Print.

"El culto a la Santísima Muerte, un boom en Mexico." *Terra Networks.* Terra, 2011. Web. October 19, 2011. http://php.terra.com/templates.

Cunha, Mariano Carneiro da. "A feitiçaria entre os Nagô-Yorubá." *Dédalo* 23 (1984): 1–16. Print.

Czaplicka, M. A. *Aboriginal Siberia: A Study in Social Anthropology.* 1914. Oxford: Clarendon, 1969. Print.

Dalmiya, Vrinda. "Loving Paradoxes: A Feminist Reclamation of the Goddess Kali." *Hypatia* 15.1 (Winter 2001): 125–50. Print.

DaMatta, Roberto. *Carnavais, malandros, e heróis: para uma sociologia do dilema brasileiro.* 5th ed. Rio de Janeiro: Guanabara, 1990. Print.

———. *A casa & a rua: espaço, cidadania, mulher e morte no Brasil.* 5th ed. Rio de Janeiro: Rocco, 1997. Print.

"Dan 66 años de cárcel a líder de Santa Muerte." *Informador.mx.* June 14, 2012. Web. February 24, 2015. http://www. informador.com.mx.

Devī-māhātmyam (Glory of the Devine Mother). 1953. Trans. Swami Jagadiswarananda. Mylapore, India: Adhyaksha, 2009. Print.

Devoción a la Santa Muerte: Altares y testimonios 3. Mexico City: Editorial Mina, 2006. Print.

D'Oxum, Dalva. *Mirongas: magia e feitiço.* 2nd ed. Rio de Janeiro: Pallas, 1991. Print.

Drewal, Henry. "Efe: Voiced Power and Pageantry." *African Arts* (1974): 26–29, 58, 66, 82–83. *JSTOR*. Web. October 3, 2012. http://www.jstor.org.

Drewal, Henry John, and Margaret Thompson Drewal. *Gẹlẹdẹ: Art and Female Power among the Yoruba*. 1990. Eds. Paula Ben-Amos, Roy Sieber, and Robert Farris Thompson. Bloomington: Indiana University Press, 1983. Print.

Erndl, Kathleen M. "The Goddess and Women's Power. A Hindu Case-Study." *Women and Goddess Traditions*. Ed. Karen L. King. Minneapolis: Fortress, 1997. 17–38. Print.

———. "The Play of the Mother: Possession and Power in Hindu Women's Goddess Rituals." Pintchman, *Women's Lives, Women's Rituals in the Hindu Tradition* 149–58. Print.

———. "A Trance Healing Session with Mātājī." *Tantra in Practice*. Ed. David Gordon White. New Jersey: Princeton University Press, 2000. 97–115. Print.

———. *Victory to the Mother: The Hindu Goddess of Northwest India in Myth, Ritual, and Symbol*. New York: Oxford University Press, 1993. Print.

Fagg, William. *Yoruba: Sculpture of West Africa*. Ed. Bryce Holcombe. New York: Knopf, 1982. Print.

Farreli, Maria Helena. *Pomba-Gira Cigana: magias de amor, sorte, sonhos, reza forte, comidas e ofrendas*. 2nd ed. Rio de Janeiro: Pallas, 2006. Print.

Flores Martos, Juan Antonio. "La Santísima Muerte en Veracruz, México: vidas descarnadas y prácticas encarnadas." Cuenca: Ediciones de la U Castilla-La Mancha, 2007. 273–304. Print.

———. "Transformismos y transculturación de un culto novomestizo emergente: la Santa Muerte mexicana." *Teorías y prácticas emergentes en antropología de la religión* 10. Ed. Mónica Cornejo, Manuela Cantón, and Ruy Llera Spain: Donostia, 2008. 55–76. Web. November 1, 2013. http://www.ankulegui.org.

Fonseca, C. Bomfim da. "A dança cigana: A construção de uma identidade cigana em um grupo de camadas médias no Rio de Janeiro." MA thesis, Universidade Federal do Rio de Janeiro, 2002. Print.

"The Forum Dedicated to Enochian and Magical Evocation: A Prayer to Pomba Gira." *Evocationmagic*. Evocation magic, June 27, 2012. Web. November 14, 2012. http://www.evocationmagic.com.

Fragoso Lugo, Perla Orquídea. "La muerte santificada: el culto a la Santa Muerte en la ciudad de México." *Revista de El Colegio de San Luis* 26–27 (2007): 9–37. Print.

Franco, Jean. The Decline and Fall of the Lettered City. Cambridge, MA and London: Harvard University Press, 2002. Print.

Frawley, David. *Tantric Yoga and the Wisdom Goddesses*. 1994. Twin Lakes, WI: Lotus Press, 2010. Print.

Frigerio, Alejandro. "Compadre en tiempos difíciles." Batalla, *Dueños de la encrucijada* n. pag. Print.
Fry, Peter. "Mediundade e sexualidade." *Religião e Sociedade* 1 (1977): 105–23. Print.
Fry, Peter Henry, and Gary Nigel Howe. "Duas respostas à aflição: umbranda e pentecostalismo." *Debate e critica* 6 (1975): 75–94. Print.
Garibay, K. Angel M, ed. *La literatura de los aztecas*. 1964. Mexico City: Mortiz, 1992. Print.
Garma, Carlos. "El culto a la Santa Muerte." *El Universal*. Universal, April 10, 2009. Web. October 19, 2011. http://www.eluniversal.com.mx.
Gaytán Alcalá, Felipe. "Santa entre los malditos. Culto a la Santa Muerte en el México del Siglo XXI." *Liminar* 6.1 (2008): 13–25. *Redalyc*. Web. November 1, 2013.
Geertz, Clifford. *The Interpretation of Cultures*. New York: Basic, 1973. Print.
Ghosha, Pratāpachandra. *Durga Puja*. Calcutta: Hindoo Patriot Press, 1871. Print.
Gil Olmos, José. *La Santa Muerte. La virgen de los olvidados*. Mexico City: Debolsillo, 2010. Print.
Gimbutas, Marija. *The Goddesses and Gods of Old Europe*. 1974. Berkeley: University of California Press, 1992. Print.
———. *The Language of the Goddess*. 1989. New York: Harper, 1991. Print.
———. *The Living Goddesses*. Berkeley: University of California Press, 1999. Print.
———. "Women and Culture in Goddess-Oriented Old Europe." Spretnak 22–31. Print.
Gliński, Antoni J. "O królewnie zaklętej w żabę." *U złotego źródła baśnie polskie*. 1968. Comp. Stefania Wortman. Warsaw: Nasza Księgarnia, 1996. 38–47. Print.
Goettner-Abendroth, Heide. *Matriarchal Societies*. New York: Peter Lang, 2012. Print.
González Rodríguez, Sergio. "Noche y día/La Santa Muerte de los criminales." *Reforma.com*. Reforma, April 28, 2001. Web. October 18, 2011. http://galegroup.com.
Graves, Robert. *The Greek Myths*. New York: Penguin, 1955. 2 Vols. Print.
Graves, Robert, and Rapael Patai. *Hebrew Myths*. Vol. 1. New York: Penguin, 1955. 2 Vols. Print.
Gupta, Sanjukta. "The Domestication of a Goddess." McDermott and Kripal, eds. *Encountering Kālī* 60–79. Print.
Gutiérrez, Tonatiuh, and Elektra. "La muerte en el arte popular mexicano." *Artesde M éxico*75–77.
Guttman, Arthemis. *Práctica del culto a la Santa Muerte*. Mexico City: Editores Mexicanos Unidos, 2009. Print.
Harding, Elizabeth U. *Kali: The Black Goddess of Dakshineswar*. York Beach: Nicolas-Hays, 1993. Print.

Harle, James C. "Durgā, Goodess of Victory." *Artibus Asiae Publishers* 26.3, 4 (1963): 237–46. Print.
Hawley, John S., and Donna M. Wulff, eds. *Devī: Goddesses of India.* Berkeley: University of California Press, 1996. Print.
———. *The Divine Consort: Rādhā and the Goddesses of India.* Berkeley: Graduate Theological Union, 1982. Print.
Hayes, K. "Fogos cruzados: a traição e os limites da possessão pela Pomba Gira. Trans. M. Souza." *Religião e Sociedade* 25.2 (2005): 82–101. Print.
Hayes, Kelly E. "The Dark Side of the Feminine: Pomba Gira Spirits in Brazil." Korieh, Chima J., and Philomina Okeke-Ihejirika, eds. *Gendering Global Transformations: Gender, Culture, Race and Identity* 2009.119–32. Print.
———. *Holy Harlots: Femininity, Sexuality, and Black Magic in Brazil.* 1968. Berkeley: University of California Press, 2011. Print.
Hernández Hernández, Alfonso. "Devoción a la Santa Muerte y San Judas Tadeo en Tepito y anexas." *El Cotidiano* 169 (2011): n. pag. Print.
Hess, David J. "Umbanda and Quimbanda Magic in Brazil." *Archives des sciences sociales des religions* 79 (1992): 135–53. Print.
Hess, David J., and Roberto A. DaMatta, eds. *The Brazilian Puzzle: Culture on the Borderlands of the Western World.* New York: Colombia University Press, 1995. Print.
Hicks, David, ed. *Ritual and Belief.* 3rd ed. Lanham and New York: Altamira Press, 2010. Print.
Hoch-Smith, Judith. "Radical Yoruba Female Sexuality: The Witch and the Prostitute." *Women in Ritual and Symbolic Roles.* Eds. Judith Hoch-Smith and A. Spring. New York: Plenum, 1978. 245–67. Print.
Horvath, Agnes. "Liminality and the Unreal Class of the Image-Making Craft: An Essay on Political Alchemy." *International Political Anthropology* 2.1 (2009): 51–73. Print.
Hubbs, Joanna. *Mother Russia: The Feminine Myth in Russian Culture.* 1988. Bloomington: Indiana University Press, 1993. Print.
Humes, Cynthia Ann. "Wrestling with Kālī." McDemont, *Encountering Kālī* 145–168. Print.
Ivanov, V., and V. Toporov. "Baba-Yaga." *Mifologicheskij slovar'.* Ed. E. M. Mieletinskij. Moscow: Sovietskaia Entsiklopedia, 1990. 85–86. Print.
Jiménez, Eugenia. "La Santa Muerte tendrá su catedral en el DF para 2010." *Milenio.* Grupo Editorial Milenio, July 15, 2009. Web. October 19,2010. http://www.milenio.com.
Johns, Andreas. *Baba Yaga: The Ambiguous Mother and Witch of the Russian Folktale.* 2004. New York: Lang, 2010. Print.
Journal. Link TV, September 12, 2014. Television.

Karpūrādi-stotra (Hymn to Kālī). Trans. Arthur Avalon. Madras: Ganesh, 1965. Print.

King, Karen, ed. *Women and Goddess Traditions*. Minneapolis: Fortress, 1997. Print.

Kinsley, David R. *Hindu Goddesses: Visions of the Divine Feminine in the Hindu Religious Tradition*. Berkeley: University of California Press, 1986. Print.

———. "Independent Goddesses: Blood and Death out of Place Reflections on the Goddess Kālī." *The Divine Consort*. Eds. John Stratton Hawley and Donna Marie Wulff. Berkeley: University of California Press, 1982. 144–52. Print.

———. *The Sword and the Flute: Kālī and Kṛṣṇa. Dark Visions of the Terrible and the Sublime in Hindu Mythology*. Berkeley: University of California Press, 1975. Print.

———. *Tantric Visions of the Divine Feminine*. Berkeley: University of California Press, 1997. Print.

Kohli, Anna. *Trzy kolory bogini*. Kraków, Poland: Wydawnictwo eFKa, 2007. Print.

Kopaliński, Władysław. *Słownik symboli*. Warsaw: Wiedza Powszechna, 1990. Print.

Korieh, Chima J., and Philomina Okeke-Ihejirika, eds. *Gendering Global Transformation: Gender, Culture, and Race*. New York: Routledge, 2009. Print.

Kramer, Heinrich, and Jacob Sprenger. *Malleus Maleficarum*. 1487. Trans. Montague Summers. 1928. Web. March 19, 2013. http://www.malleusmaleficarum.org.

Kravchenko, Maria. *The World of the Russian Fairy Tale*. Berne: Lang, 1987. Print.

Kṛṣṇānanda Āgamavāgīśa. *Bṛhat Tantrasāra*. Calcutta: Navabharat Publishers, 1984. Print.

Kuersteiner, Albert F., ed. *Poesías del Canciller Pedro López de Ayala*. Vol. 2. New York: The Hispanic Society of America, 1920. Print.

Landes, Ruth. *The City of Women*. 1947. Albuquerque: University of New Mexico Press, 1994. Print.

———. "Fetish Worship in Brazil." *American Folklore* 53.210 (1940): 261–70. Print.

León-Portilla, Miguel. *Los antiguos mexicanos a través de sus crónicas y cantares*. 1961. Mexico City: Fondo de Cultura Económica, 1970. Print.

Lerch, Patricia B. "An Explanation for the Predominance of Women in the Umbanda Cults of Porto Alegre, Brazil." *Urban Anthropology* 2.2 (1982): 237–61. Print.

Leslie, Julia, ed. *Roles and Rituals for Hindu Women*. Delhi: Motilal Banarsidass Publishers, 1992. Print.

———. "Śrī and Jyeṣṭā: Ambivalent Role Models for Women." Julia Leslie, ed. *Roles and Rituals for Hindu Women* 107–27. Print.

"Líder de la iglesia de la Santa Muerte recibe 12 años de cárcel." *Informador.mx.*, September 14, 2011. Web. February 24, 2015. http://www.informador.com.mx.

MacDermott, Mercia. *Bulgarian Folk Customs.* London and Philadelphia: Jessica Kingsley Publishers, 1998. Print.

MacKay, Christopher S. *The Hammer of Witches: A Complete Translation of Malleus Maleficarum.* 2009. Cambridge: Cambridge University Press, 2011. Print.

Maggie, Yvonne. *Medo do feitiço: relações entre magia e poder no Brasil.* Rio de Janeiro: Arquivo Nacional, 1992. Print.

The Magic Ring: Russian Folktales from Alexander Afanasiev's Collection. 1985. Moscow: Raduga, 2001. Print.

Mahānirvāna Tantra (Tantra of the Great Liberation). Trans. Arthur Avalon. New York: Dover, 1972. Print.

Malvido, Elsa. "Crónicas de la Buena Muerte y la Santa Muerte en México." *Arqueología Mexicana.* January 10, 2006: 20–27. Print.

———"El mexicano y el concepto de la muerte." *Las caras de la muerte en el mundo.* Ed. Sonia Butze. Mexico City: INAH, 1996. n. pag. Print.

Manushi: Women Bhakta Poets. 50, 51, 52 (1989). Print.

Marcondes de Carlos Eugênio. ed. *Candomblé: Religião do corpo e da alma.* 2000. Rio de Janeiro: Pallas, 2004. Print.

Marinis, Valerie De. "With Dance and Drum: A Psycho-Cultural Investigation of the Meaning-Making System of an African-Brazilian Macumba Community in Salvador, Brazil." Clarke, *New Trends and Developments in African Religions*, 1998. 59–73. Print.

Martín, Desirée A. *Borderlands Saints.* New Brunswick, NJ : Rutgers University Press, 2014. Print.

Martin, John. Personal interview. October 20, 2012.

Martine, George, and Gordon McGranahan. *Brazil's Early Urban Transition: What Can It Teach Urbanizing Countries?* London and New York: IIED and UNFPA, 2010. Print.

Matory, J. Lorand. *Black Atlantic Religion.* Princeton: Princeton University Press, 2005. Print.

Matos Moctezuma, Eduardo, ed. *Artes de México. Miccaihuitl: El Culto a la Muerte.* Mexico: n.p., 1971. Print.

Matos Moctezuma, Eduardo. "La muerte en el México prehispánico." *Artesde México* 6–9. Print.

McDaniel, J. "Does Tantric Ritual Empower Women? Renunciation and Domesticity among Female Tantrikas." Pintchman, *Women's Lives, Women's Rituals in the Hindu Tradition* 159–75. Print.

———. *Offering Flowers, Feeding Skulls: Popular Goddess Worship in West Bengal.* Oxford: Oxford University Press, 2004. Print.

McDermott, Rachel Fell, and Jeffrey J. Kripal, eds. *Encountering Kālī: In the Margins, at the Center, in the West.* Berkeley: University of California Press, 2003. Print.
McNeal, Keith E. "Doing the Mother's Caribbean Work: On *Shakti* and Society in Contemporary Trinidad." McDermott, *Encountering Kālī* 223–48. Print.
Mérimée, P. *Carmen.* Trans. H. Barrera Orrego. Bogotá: Norma, 1990. Print.
Meyer, Marlyse. *Maria Padilha e toda a sua quadrilha: de amante de um rei de Castela a Pomba-Gira de Umbanda.* Sao Paulo: Duas Cidades, 1993. Print.
Meza Márquez, Consuelo. "Discurso literario de las poetas garífunas del Caribe centroamericano: Honduras, Nicaragua y Guatemala." *Latinoamérica. Revista de Estudios Latinoamericanos* 55 (2012): 245–78. Web. May 12, 2013. http://www.redalyc.org.
Michaels, Axel, Cornelia Vogelsanger, and Annette Wilke, eds. *Wild Goddesses in India and Nepal: Proceedings of an International Symposium.* Berne and Zurich 1994. Berlin: Lang, 1996. Print.
Michalik, Piotr Grzegorz. "The Meaning of Death: Semiotic Approach to Analysis of Syncretic Processes in the Cult of Santa Muerte." N.d. TS. Institute of Religious Studies, Jagiellonian University, Kraków, Poland. Print.
Miłosz, Oskar. "Królowa węży." *Baśnie i legendy litewskie.* Olsztyn: Pojezierze, 1986. 91–98. Print.
Molina, N. A. *Saravá Pomba Gira.* Rio de Janeiro: Espiritualista, n.d. Print.
Montero, Paula. *Da Doenca à Desordem: A Magia na Umbanda.* Rio de Janeiro: Graal, 1985. Print.
Moura, Carlos Eugenio Marcondes de, comp. *Candomblé: religião do corpo e da alma.* 2000. Rio de Janeiro: Pallas, 2004. Print.
Nagaswamy, R. *Tantric Cult of South India.* Delhi: Agam Kala Prakashan, 1982. Print.
Nascimento, Adriano Roberto Afonso do, Lidio de Souza, and Zeidi Araújo Trindade. "Exus e Pombas-Giras: O Masculino e o Femenino nos Puntos Cantados da Umbanda." *Psicologia em Estudo, Maringá* 6.2 (2001): 107–13. Print.
Navarrete, Carlos. *San Pascualito Rey y el culto a la muerte en Chiapas.* Mexico City: UNAM, 1982. Print.
Negrão, Lísias Nogueira. *Entre a Cruz e a Encruzilhada: formação de Campo Umbadista em São Paulo.* Sao Paulo: Edusp, 1996. Print.
Nivedita, Sister. *Kali the Mother.* Mayavati: Ashrama, 1950. Print.
Noticiero Noc turno U nivisión. Univisión, October 20, 2012. Television.
———. Univisión, November 3, 2013. Television.
Obeyesekere, Ranjini, and Gananath Obeyesekere. "The Tale of the Demoness Kālī : A Discourse on Evil." *History of Religions* 29.4 (May

1990): 318–34. *JSTOR*. Web. September 23, 2010. http://links.jstor.org.
Obregón, Gonzalo. "Representación de la muerte en el arte colonial." *Artesde M éxico* 37–39. Print.
Oleszkiewicz, Eligiusz. Personal interview. June 19, 2013.
Oleszkiewicz-Peralba, Małgorzata. *The Black Madonna in Latin America and Europe: Tradition and Transformation.* 2007. Albuquerque: University of New Mexico Press, 2009. Print.
———. "El narcotráfico y la religión en América Latina." *Revista del CESLA* 13.1 (2010): 211–24. Print.
———. "Representations of Death in Mexico: La Santa Muerte." *Proceedings of the Art of Death & Dying Symposium Held at the University of Houston (TX), October 25–27, 2012.* Houston: University of Houston Libraries, 2013. 69–77. Web. November 4, 2013. http://journals.tdl.org.
———. "Saint Sara La-Kâli: The Romani Black Madonna." *She is Everywhere!* Vol. 3. Eds. Mary Saracino and Mary Beth Moser. Bloomington: iUniverse, 2012. 128–43. Print.
———. "Święta Śmierć, Nasza Opiekunka: Meksykańska Santa Muerte/Holy Death, Our Protectress: The Mexican Santa Muerte." *Etnografia nowa/The New Ethnography* 5 (2013): 119–39. Print.
Omolubá. *Maria Molambo na sombra e na luz.* 10th ed. Sao Paulo: Cristális,2002.P rint.
Ortiz, Renato. *A Morte Branca do Feiticeiro Negro.* Petrópolis: Vozes, 1978. Print.
Osorno, Diego Enrique. *La guerra de los Zetas. Viaje por la frontera de la narcopolítica.* Mexico City: Grijalbo, 2012. Print.
Pagels, Elaine. *The Gnostic Gospels.* 1979. New York: Vintage, 1989. Print.
Parker, Richard. "Masculinity, Femininity, and Homosexuality: On the Anthropological Interpretation of Sexual Meanings in Brazil." *Journal of Homosexuality* 11.3–4 (1985): 155–63. Print.
Patai, Raphael. *The Hebrew Goddess.* N.p. (USA): Ktav Publishing House, Inc., 1967. Print.
Perdigón Castañeda, J. Katia. *La Santa Muerte protectora de los hombres.* Mexico City: UNAM, 2008. Print.
Pereira, Cristina da Costa. *Povos de rua.* Rio de Janeiro: Luziletras, 2003. Print.
Pereira, Mariana Figueiredo de Castro. "A evolução habitacional-urbana na cidade de Rio de Janeiro." *Em Debate* 8 (2009). Web. April 28, 2014. http://wwwmaxwell. lambda.ele.puc-rio.br.
Perkowska, Ewa. *Złota Baba.* N.d. TS. Jacek Dobrowolski collection, Warsaw. Print.

"Pharmacy." *Online Etymology Dictionary.* Web. December 23, 2014. http://www.etymoline.com.
Pintchman, Tracy, ed. *Seeking Mahādevī: Constructing the Identities of the Hindu Great Goddess.* New York: State University of New York Press, 2001. Print.
———. *Women's Lives, Women's Rituals in the Hindu Tradition.* New York: Oxford University Press, 2001. Print.
Los poderes mágicos de la Santa Muerte. Mexico: Ediciones S.M, n.d. Print.
Pott, P. H. "The Sacred Cemeteries of Nepal." *Yoga and Yantra.* Ed. P. H. Pott. The Hague: Martinus Nijhoff, 1966. 76–101. Print.
Potter, Stephen, and Laurens Sargent. "Nature and the Gods." *Pedigree: The Origins of Words from Nature.* New York: Taplinger, 1974. 197–203. Print.
Prandi, Reginaldo. "African Gods in Contemporary Brazil: A Sociological Introduction to Candomblé Today." *International Sociology* 15.4 (2000): 641–63. Web. October 20, 2011. http://sagepublications.com.
———. "Exu de Mensageiro à Diabo." *RevistaUSP.* Revista USP, n.d. Web. October 19, 2011. http://candomble.i8.com.
———. "Pombagiras dos candomblés e umbandas as faces inconfessas do Brasil." *Revista brasileira de ciências sociais* 26.9 (1994): 91–102. Print.
Proceedings of the Art of Death & Dying Symposium Held at the University of Houston (TX), October 25–27, 2012. Web. November 4, 2013. http://journals.tdl.org/add/index.php/add/index.
"Projeto Cidadania de Ciganos e Nômades é lançado na ALMG." *Assembleia de Minas Gerais* (2009): n. pag. Print.
Propp, Vladimir. *Morfología del cuento.* 1972. Trans. Lourdez Ortiz. Madrid: Fundamentos, 1981. Print.
———. *Las raíces históricas del cuento.* Trans. José Martín Arancibia, 1974. Madrid: Fundamentos, 1981. Print.
———. "Las transformaciones de los cuentos maravillosos." Propp, *Morfología del cuento* 153–78.
Puja: Expressions of Hindu Devotion. Narr. Arthur M. Sockeer Gallery. Smithsonian Institution, Wasington, DC, 1996. Videocassette.
Ramirez, K. [Kelli Cristine Lopes Rego]. Personal interview. June 7, 2009.
Rego, Waldeloir. "Mitos e Ritos Africanos da Bahia." Carybé, *Iconografia* 269–77. Print.
Rey-Henningsen, Marisa. *The World of the Ploughwoman.* Helsinki: Suomalainen. Tiedeakatemia Academia Scientiarum Fennica, 1994. Print. FF Communications 254. Print.
Ribeiro, José. *Eu, Maria Padilha.* 4th ed. Rio de Janeiro: Pallas, 2006. Print.
Rigoglioso, Marguerite. *The Cult of Divine Birth in Ancient Greece.* New York: Palgrave, 2009. Print.

———. *Virgin Mother Goddesses of Antiquity.* New York: Palgrave, 2010. Print.
"Rio de Janeiro World Peace Crusade." *Articlebase.* Article Base, n.d. Web. http://www.articlesbase.com.
Rishi, Padmashri W. R. *Roma.* Patiala: Punjabi University, 1966. Print.
———. "Sati Sara Consort of God Shiva." *Roma* 3 (1977): 4–7. Print.
Romancero general, en que se contienen todos los Romances que andan impressos en las nueve partes de Romancero. Ed. Luis Sanchez. Madrid: 1600. Print.
Roush, Laura. "Santa Muerte, Protection, and *Desamparo.*" *Latin American Research Review* 49 (2014): 129–48. Print.
Ruiz Guadalajara, Juan Carlos. "Religiosidad en movimiento." *Revista de El Colegio de San Luis* 26–27 (2007): 5–8. Print.
Ruiz Parra, Emiliano. "Divide a fieles la Santa Muerte." *ElNorte.com.* El Norte, February 21, 2005. Web. October 18, 2011. http://galegroup.com.
Ruiz, Paula. "Ahora será Cartel de Santa...Muerte." *ElNorte.com.* El Norte, March 8, 2008. Web. October 18, 2011. http://galegroup.com.
Sahagún, Fray Bernardino de. *Florentine Codex: General History of the Things of New Spain,* Bk. 1. Trans. Charles E. Dibble and Arthur J. O. Anderson. Santa Fe: School for American Research; Salt Lake City: University of Utah, 1950. Print.
Salazar, Mónica. "Teresa Margolles and the Embodiment of Absence." *Symposium Art of Death and Dying.* University of Houston, Houston, October 25, 2012. Conference.
Samanta, Suchitra. "'The Self-Animal' and Divine Digestion: Goat Sacrifice to the Goddess Kālī in Bengal." *The Journal of Asian Studies* 53.3 (August 1994): 779–803. 2 JSTOR. Web. September 23, 2010. http://links.jstor.org.
"Santa Muerte, 'narcoaltares' de Tamaulipas." *El Siglo de Torreón.* October 27, 2007. Web. April 21, 2014. mhtml:file//C:\Users\ctr120\Desktop\ Santa Muerte, 'narcoaltares' de Tamaulipas_siglo.mht.
Santana, Ernesto, comp. *Orações umbandistas de todos os tempos.* 3rd ed. Ed. Ernesto Santana. Rio de Janeiro: Pallas, 1992. Print.
Santos, Juana Elbein. dos, dir. *Iyá-mi agbá.* SECNEB, n.d. Videocassette.
———. *Osn àgôe a morte.* 7th ed. Petrópolis: Vozes, 1993. Print.
Sarlo, Beatriz. *Escenas de la vida posmoderna.* Buenos Aires, Argentina: Ariel, 1994. Print.
Sen, Rāmprasād. *Gace and Mercy in Her Wild Hair: Selected Poems to the Mother Goddess.* Trans. Leonard Nathan and Clinton Seely. Boulder, CO: Great Eastern. 1982. Print.
Shapiro, Michael, ed. "Baba-Jaga: A Search for Mythopoetic Origins and Affinities." *International Journal of Linguistics and Poetics* 27 (1983): 109–35. Print.

Singer, Isaac Bashevis. *The King of the Fields*. 1988. Trans. Isaac Bashevis Singer. New York: Penguin, 1990. Print.

———. *Stories for Children*. 1962. New York: Farrar. 1985. Print.

Sinha, Jadunath. *Rama Prasada's Devotional Songs: The Cult of Shakti*. Calcutta: Sinha, 1966. Print.

Sjöö, Monica. *The Great Cosmic Mother*. 1987. San Francisco: Harper San Francisco, 1991. Print.

"Spinosaurus Was Part Duck, Part Crocodile." *San Antonio Express News*. September 12, 2014. Print.

Spretnak, Charlene, ed. *The Politics of Women's Spirituality*. New York: Anchor Press, 1982. Print.

Stanescon, Miriam. Personal interview. May 23, 2009.

———. Telephone interview. April 26, 2009.

Szafrański, Włodzimierz. *Prahistoria religii na ziemiach polskich*. Wrocław, Poland: Ossolineum, 1987. Print.

Szakolczai, Arpad. "Liminality and Experience: Structuring Transitory Situations and Transformative Events." *International Political Anthropology* 2.1 (2009): 141–72. Print.

Szyjewski, Andrzej. *Religia Słowian*. 2003. Kraków: WAM, 2010. Print.

Tatar, Maria, ed. and trans. *The Annotated Classic Fairy Tales*. New York and London: Norton, 2002. Print.

Taussig, Michael T., ed. *The Devil and Commodity Fetishism in South America*. Chapel Hill: University of North Carolina Press, 1980. Print.

Tavárez, David. "Escritura, espacios sociales y cosmologías indígenas en Nueva España: una aproximación a los calendarios zapotecos." *Revista de Indias* 247 (2009): 39–62. Web. October 31, 2013. http://www.revistadeindias.revistas.csic.es.

Taylor, Patrick, ed. *Nation Dance*. Bloomington: Indiana University Press, 2001. Print.

Teixeira, Alves Neto. *Pomba-Gira: Enchantments to Invoke the Formidable Powers of the Female Messenger of the Gods*. Trans. Carol L. Dow. Burbank: Technicians of the Sacred, 1990. Print.

Teixeira (neto), Antônio Alves. *Pomba Gira: as duas faces da Umbanda*. Rio de Janeiro: Eco, 1966. Print.

Thomassen, Bjorn. "The Uses and Meanings of Liminality." *International Political Anthropology* 2.1 (2009): 5–27. Print.

Thompson, Ginger. "On Mexico's Mean Streets, the Sinners Have a Saint." *New York Times*. March 26, 2004. ProQuest Historical Newspapers: The New York Times (1851–2009): A4. Web. April 26, 2014.

"The Thunder Perfect Mind." *The Nag Hamadi Library in English*. Trans. Members of the Coptic Gnostic Library Project of the Institute for Antiquity and Christianity. New York: Harper, 1977. Print.

Toporov, V. N. "Khettskaia ^{SAL}ŠU.GI i slavianskaia Baba-Yaga." *Kratkie soobshchenija Instituta Slavianovedenija* 38 (1963): 28–37. Print.

Trinidade, Liana. *Exu poder e perigo.* Sao Paulo: Icone, 1985. Print.
Turner, V.W. *The Drums of Affliction.* Oxford: Oxford University Press, 1968. Print.
Turner, Victor. *Dramas, Fields, and Metaphors.* 1974. Ithaca and London: Cornell University Press, 1975. Print.
———. *The Forest of Symbols.* Ithaca, NY: Cornell University Press, 1967. Print.
———. "Liminal to Liminoid in Play, Flow, and Ritual: An Essay in Comparative Symbology." *Rice University Studies* 60.3 (1974): 53–92. Print.
———. *The Ritual Process: Structure and Anti-structure.* 1969. New Brunswick: Aldine, 2009. Print.
Umbanda: The Problem Solver. Prod. and Dir. Stephen Cross. Public Media Films, Inc., 1977–1991. Videocassette.
Van Gennep, Arnold. *The Rites of Passage.* 1908. Trans. Monika B Vizedom and Gabrielle L. Caffee. Chicago, IL: University of Chicago Press, 1960. Print.
Vargas, Alberto. "La muerte vista por el mexicano de hoy." *Artes de México* 57–59. Print.
Velázquez, Oriana. *El libro de la Santa Muerte.* Mexico City: Eds. Mex. Unidos, 2006. Print.
Verger, P. "Grandeur et décadence du culte de Iyámi Òsòròngà." *Société des Africanistes* 35.1 (1965): 141–243. Print.
Vidal, Marcelo João [Anrez Ramirez]. Personal interview. June 7, 2009.
Wadley, Susan S. "Women and the Hindu Tradition." *Signs* 3.1 (1977): 113–25. *JSTOR.* Web. February 11, 2010. http://jstor.org.
Walker, Barbara G. *The Crone.* San Francisco: Harper & Row, 1985. Print.
———. *The Woman's Dictionary of Symbols and Sacred Objects.* New York: Harper, 1988. Print.
———. *The Woman's Encyclopedia of Myths and Secrets.* New York: Harper, 1983. Print.
Walker, Sheila. "Candomblé: A Spiritual Microcosm of Africa." *Black Art* 5 (1984): 10–22. Print.
Washington, Teresa N. *Our Mothers, Our Powers, Our Texts.* Bloomington: Indiana University Press, 2005. Print.
West-Durán,Al an,e d. *Cuba.* Detroit: Gale, 2012. Print.
White, David Gordon, ed. *Tantra in Practice.* New Jersey: Princeton University Press, 2000. Print.
Wortman, Stefania, comp. *U złotego źródła baśnie polskie.* 1968. Warsaw: Nasza Księgarnia, 1996. Print.
Wosien, Maria-Gabrielle. *The Russian Folk-Tale: Some Structural and Thematic Aspects.* Munich, Germany: Verlag Otto Sagner, 1969. Print.

Index

Note: Italic page numbers refer to figures and tables.

Afanas'ev, Aleksandr, 15, 24, 36
African/African-derived religions
  in Brazil, 70, 71, 77, 83, 87–8, 90, 92, *93*
  colors in, 30–1, 83
  Exu as mediator between worlds, 33, 86–7
  and women identified as witches, 151n32
  see also Candomblé religion; pan-African belief systems; Umbanda religion
ambiguity
  and Baba Yaga, 16, 69, 137, 141
  and Kālī, 61, 69, 137, 141
  and Pombagira, 74–5, 85, 100, 134, 137, 141
  and Santa Muerte, 120, 134, 137, 141
Andrew, Saint, 33
animals
  as Baba Yaga's helpers, 20, 30, 35, 37
  dragons associated with, 28–9, 145n22
  ritual animal sacrifice, 61, 73, 89, 152n39
  see also specific animals
Annunciation of Our Lady, 33
Anthony, Saint, 154n9
Aphrodite (Greek goddess), 25
Argentina, 72, 127, 152n51
Aridjis, Eva, 153n4, 154n10
Aridjis, Homero, 113
Arlechino (Italy), 72

Augras, Monique, 72, 152n49
Avatar (film), 33
Àwọn Ìyá Wa (African ancestral mothers), 39, 73, 74–5, 76, 84, 93, 94, 98
axis mundi, 40, 49
Aztecs, deities of, 2, *2*, 27, 34, 61, 75, 127, *128*, 143n2, 156n32

Baba Marta (Martenitsa), 31–2, *32*
Baba Yaga
  and ambiguity, 16, 69, 137, 141
  animals as helpers of, 20, 30, 35, 37
  and Baba Marta, 31–2
  bird features of, 17, 23, 25, 35, 36, 51
  blindness of, 22
  bone remains associated with, 37, 61, 137
  as cannibal mother, 19
  characteristics of, 7, 16–17, 44, 45
  cremation practices associated with, 37–8
  death associated with, 7, 9, 16, 17–18, 23, 26, 30, 37, 43, 57, 58, 69, 137, 141
  and Dhūmāvatī, 19, 37–8, 57–8
  dragon as alter ego of, 28, 29–30
  duality of, 7, 17, 51, 61, 98
  dwelling places of, 9, 17, 18
  in fairy tales, 6, 7, 15, 17–20, 52, 138, 141–2
  as fierce feminine divinity, 1
  fighter aspect of, 17, 20, 44, 45

Baba Yaga—*Continued*
  formula in tales, 20–1, 37,
    144–5n10, 145n11
  as goddess of life, death, and
    regeneration, 7, 15, 17, 19, 34
  as guardian of Waters of Life and
    of Death, 18, 144n3
  hut of, 7, 9, 16, 18–19, 24, 25,
    28, 35–41, 57, 61, 137, 138,
    144n4, 146n31
  iconography of, 2, 7, 16
  illustration by Maya Sokovic, *16*
  and Kālī, 8, 15, 17, 37–8, 61,
    62–3
  liminality of, 7, 9, 15–17, 19, 36,
    39, 69, 133, 137, 138
  magical objects of, 30
  and marginality, 1, 3, 5, 9, 39,
    138, 141, 142
  as mediator, 137
  names of, 22–4, 26, 145n13
  and Pombagira, 8, 15, 74
  as pre-Slavic goddess, 7, 15, 17, 25
  Slavic folktales of, 18, 19, 20,
    22, 30, 33, 35, 36, 38, 39, 40,
    43–4, 44, 137, 144n7
  stones associated with, 45–6
  studies of, 143n10
  treasures of, 18–19, 28, 62, 77, 133
  as witch, 35, 41–5, 51–2
barô, 79, *80*
bears, 33, 35
Bengal, 60–1
Benin, 93
Bhadrakālī (Hindu goddess), 42–3
birch trees, 39–40
bird goddesses, 24–6, 27, 28
birds
  bird features of Baba Yaga, 17,
    23, 25, 35, 36, 51
  bird features of Dhūmāvatī, 58,
    145n17
  as mediators, 20, 26–7
  in Polish paper cutouts, 49, *49*
  and Slavic traditions, 25, 97
  snakes associated with, 27
  as totems, 21, 32
  and Yoruba religion, 95, 97
Bizet, Georges, 77
Black Goddess, 17
Black Madonna, Einsiedeln,
  Switzerland, 66
*The Black Madonna in Latin
  America and Europe*
  (Oleszkiewicz-Peralba), 1
Boas, Franz, 23–4
Bolaños, Joaquín, 156–7n36
Bombonjira, 8, 72
Borbón, Blanca de, 77
Botánica Papa Jim's, San Antonio,
  Texas, *109*, 115, *116*
botánicas, *109*, 111–12, 115–16,
  116, *117*, 154n13
Brazil
  African slave groups brought to,
    148–9n5
  African/African-derived religions
    in, 70, 71, 77, 83, 87–8, 90,
    92, *93*
  favelas of, 4, 100, 153n52
  immigrant population of, 151n30
  Kali Sara procession in, 65
  outsiders of, 6–7
  Roma in, 83, 150–1n27
  syncretic religions in, 70–1, 78–9
  see also Pombagira
Bruegel, Pieter, the Elder, 155n29
Brumana, Eduardo Giobellina, 88
bruxas, 93, 98, 132, 152n42
  see also witches
Bulgaria
  dragons in, 30
  house snakes in, 27
  Martenitsas, *32*
Byelorussia, 23, 27

Caboclos, 80
La Calavera Catrina (Elegant Lady),
  129–30
Calderón, Felipe, 119
Caldwell, Sarah, 143n10
Campbell, Joseph, 27

INDEX 177

Candomblé religion
 benign female divinities of, 1
 casa de força (house of strength) in, 40
 continuum of, *93*
 goddess as trinity in, 34
 and Iemanjá, 135, 152n49
 matriarchal organization of, 71
 offerings of, 89
 orixás of, 70, 74, 84, 86, 87, 90, 100, 101, 147n5, 148n3, 149n8
 priestly function performed by women, 147n37
 and Mesa Branca ceremonies, 152n41
 re-Africanization of, 71, 93, *93*
 and religious communities, 87
 and syncretism, 79
 and trances, 151n38
 and Yoruba slaves, 148–9n5
Capone, Stefania, 92
Cárdenas, Lázaro, 130
Case, Frederick Ivor, 148n9
Catalonia, *Tapís de la creació* (Tapestry of Creation), 23, *24*
Catholic Church
 and Candomblé religion, 71
 and death, 124, 129, 155n27
 evangelization by, 139
 Holy Inquisition, 93, 126
 and Santa Muerte, 112, 113, 116, 118
 and Sara Kali, 65, 78, 149n6
 and Sara-La-Kâli, 64
 and Umbanda religion, 78, 79, 88, 93, 134
 see also Virgin Mary
ceiba tree, 145n21, 152n43
Celts, 25
Center of Gypsy Studies (CEC), Brazil, 150–1n27
Chesnut, Andrew, 143n10, 153n4, 154n10
Chhandogya Upanishad, 31
children's games, 5, 22, 141

Chopin, Fryderyk, 147n41
Christianity
 Devil as intermediary between worlds, 33
 and dragons, 30, 145n23
 extremes of Virgin Mary and Eve, 150n18
 and Holy Communion, 21
 Holy Spirit as dove, 25–6
 and horses, 33
 snakes demonized in, 30
 and Virgin Mary's guardianship of cities, 145n19
 women excluded from religious posts, 43
 see also Catholic Church; Virgin Mary
Ciganos (Gypsies), 78–9, *79*
 see also Roma
Cihuateteo (Aztec women deified by death in childbirth), 127, *128*, 156n32
Cipriano, Perly, 150n27
Ciuacoatl (Aztec goddess), 27
Coatlicue
 as Aztec Mother Goddess, 143n2
 iconography of, 2, *2*, 61, 127
coconut, Kālī associated with, 66, 148n9
colonias, 4, 8, 103, 114
colors
 of Kālī, 75
 of Pombagira, 8, 75, 83, 86, 91, 108, 133–4
 sacred colors, 30–2, 33, 34
 of Santa Muerte, 108, 110–11, 123, 127, 134
Contins, Marcia, 100
coyote, 72
Cros Sandoval, Mercedes, 152n47
cults, concept of, 9, 143n9
Cunha, Mariano Carneiro da, 98
curanderos, 115, 154n12
Czech Republic, 23, 27

Day of the Dead, 132, 156–7n36
death
　Altars for the Dead, *129*, 130, 131–2, *131*
　Baba Yaga associated with, 7, 9, 16, 17–18, 23, 26, 30, 37, 43, 57, 58, 69, 137, 141
　bird goddess associated with, 25
　black death of Middle Ages, 125
　and Catholic Church, 124, 129, 155n27
　death chariots, 125–6, 156n30
　divine feminine's power over, 1
　dragons associated with, 28
　imagery of, 9, 125–30, *128*, 155n29
　Irmandade de Boa Morte, Cachoeira, Bahia, Brazil, 155n27
　Kālī associated with, 54, 56, 57, 59, 61–2, 69, 137, 141
　and liminality, 5
　in Mexican arts and folklore, 129–32
　in Mexican literature, 156–7n36
　in Mexican society, 118–23
　Pombagira associated with, 76, 99, 133–4, 137, 141
　Santa Muerte as, 9, 10, 118–19, 123, 137, 141
Devī-māhātmyam (Glory of the Divine Mother), 96, 157n1
devotees
　and hidden dimensions of reality, 141
　of Kālī, 56, 61, 63, 139
　marginalization of, 9
　methods of, 111–14
　of Pombagira, 63, 70, 134, 139
　resilience of, 142
　of Santa Muerte, 63, 106, 107, 108, 112, 113, 115, 116–17, 118, 119, 120, 122, 123, 134, 139
　and syncretism, 134
　and trances, 63
devotional centers
　of Pombagira, 78–81, 152n51
　of Santa Muerte, 114–18, 155n26
devotions
　demonization of, 139
　to Kālī, 52, 62, 64, 66, 140–1
　methods of, 111–14
　official devotions, 140
　to Pombagira, 63, 70, 132, 140
　to Santa Muerte, 10, 103, 104, 105, 106, 107–8, 111–14, 115, 116, 117–18, 119, 120, 121–3, 132, 133, 139, 140, 155n24, 155n25
　to Sara-La-Kâli, 108
Dhūmāvatī
　and Baba Yaga, 19, 37–8, 57–8
　bird features of, 58, 145n17
　cremation practices associated with, 38
　Kālī connected to, 8
　as Mahāvidyā, 54
　necklace of severed heads, 55
divine feminine
　embodying liminality, 1, 3, 5
　embodying marginality, 3, 5
　embodying outsiderhood, 1, 2, 6
　sweetening (dulcification) of, 5, 6, 60–1, 62, 66, 84, 99, 100, 134–5, 141
　see also dulcification; *and specific goddesses*
dolls, 19, 144n7
Donizetti, Gaetano, 77
dragons
　animals associated with, 28–9, 145n22
　as Baba Yaga's alter ego, 28, 29–30, 35
　characteristics of, 28
　and Christianity, 30, 145n23
　as guardians of Waters of Life, 28
　as mediators, 20
　as symbols of Mother Earth, 26

drug trafficking, Santa Muerte
associated with, 9, 113, 118,
119, 138
dulcification
of divine feminine, 100, 141
of Iemanjá, 84, *84*, 100
of Kālī, 6
see also sweetening (dulcification)
Durer, Albert, 155n29
Durgā Pūjā, 64, 138, 149n6

É hešta (house of bones), 18
earth goddess
treasures of, 18–19
see also Holy Mother Earth;
Mother Moist Earth
Eastern Europe, 5
Eastern healing practices, 79
Eguns, 90, 97, 98
Egypt, 144n7
empowerment, 8, 59, 63, 64, 71, 74, 93, 147n5
Empusae (female demons), 140
entidades
Pombagira as, 63, 147n5
of Umbanda religion, 90–1
Erndl, Kathleen M., 74
Etugen (Mongolian Earth Goddess), 42
European Middle Ages, 125
Ewa (iabá), 73
Explode coração (telenovela), 83
Exu
agency of, 101
Bombonjira as Congo name for, 8
colors of, 83, 86, 91, 127
image made of coconut shell, 148n9
liminality of, 92
and male sexual power, 98
as mediator, 33, 86–7
representation of, *86*
as street spirit, 91, *91*, 92
symbols of, *81*, *82*
and Umbanda religion, 79, 85–6, 87, 88, 91, 97
and Yoruba religion, 72

fairy tales
Baba Yaga in, 6, 7, 15, 17–20, 52, 138, 141–2
Baba Yaga's hut in, 35–41
divine feminine in, 5
dolls in, 19, 144n7
dragon as alter ego of Baba Yaga, 28
horses in, 33
favelas, 4, 100, 153n52
fierce feminine archetypes, 10
fish, and Yoruba religion, 95
fragmentation
and Baba Yaga, 16–17, 18, 57, 120, 137
and Kālī, 55, 57, 120, 137
and Pombagira, 137
and Santa Muerte, 137
frogs, 35, 146n29

Garífuna (Honduras), 147n37
Geertz, Clifford, 43
Germany, 21, 23
Gimbutas, Marija, 25, 27, 36, 145n16
Goettner-Abendroth, Heide, 147n38
Goldman, Marcio, 100
Gorgon/Medusa (Greek goddess), 27
Great Mother, 58, 137, 157n1
Greek Orthodox Church, 28
griffins, 29
Guadalupe
and Chicano/a artists in US, 154–5n21
icons in botánicas, 115, *116*
as "official" saint, 139
Santa Muerte as, 110, *111*
Sante Muerte compared to, 112, 119, 120
and syncretism, 134
Guaraní Indians, 127
Guatemala, 126, 127, 144n7
Guhyakālī (Hindu goddess), 27
Guyana, 65–6, 141, 148n9
Gypsies. *See* Roma

Harding, Elizabeth U., 143n10
Hayes, Kelly, 81, 100, 143n10

Hermes (Greek god), 72
Hernandez, Ester, 154–5n21
Hinduism, 31
  see also Kālī
Hittites, 18–19, 37, 144n6
Holbein, Hans, 155n29
holy harlots and prostitutes, 8, 70, 74, 75, 89, 100, 148n2
Holy Mother Earth, 46, 51
horses
  of Baba Yaga, 20, 33, 35, 45
  as intermediaries between worlds, 33–4
  wild horses as totems, 21, 32

Iansã/Oyá (iabá), 73, 84, 97
Iemanjá/Yemayá (queen of the oceans)
  public feast for, 152n49
  sacrifices for, 73
  and Santa Muerte, 107
  sweetening (dulcification) of, 84, *84*, 99, 100, 134–5, 141
  syncretism with Virgin Mary, 84
  and Yoruba religion, 34
Iglesia Tradicional México-Estados Unidos, Mexico City, 114, 115
Inanna (Sumerian goddess), 58
Indian diaspora, and Kālī, 5, 7, 64–6
Ishtar, Mother of Harlots, 148n2
Isis (Egyptian goddess), 46, 58, 146n29
Islam, 43
Ìyàmi Òṣoròngà
  Baba Yaga compared to, 17, 20, 30, 146n24
  and birds, 25
  feminine divinities assuming form of, 97
  invocation of, 87
  Kālī compared to, 58, 59, 62
  Pombagira associated with, 8, 75, 98–9

Jayamkondar, *Kālīngattuparani*, 57
Jesus Christ
  Oxalá syncretized with, 79, 149n8
  on Tzara Ramirez, Rio de Janeiro, Brazil altar, *78*
Johns, Andreas, 143n10
Judaism, 43
Judas Tadeo, San, 112, 119
Justo Juez (Just Judge), 126

Kālī
  and ambiguity, 61, 69, 137, 141
  and Baba Yaga, 8, 15, 17, 37–8, 61, 62–3
  cremation grounds associated with, 9, 38, 56, 59, 75, 137
  devotions to, 52, 62, 64, 66, 140–1
  duality of, 61, 98
  dwelling place of, 8, 9, 10, 137
  as fierce feminine divinity, 1, 53–4
  iconography of, 2, 58–61
  illustration by Maya Sokovic, *60*
  and Indian diaspora, 5, 7, 64–6
  liminality of, 69, 133, 137, 138
  and marginality, 1, 3, 5, 9, 54, 55, 56–7, 66, 138, 140–1, 142
  as mediator, 137
  necklace of severed heads, 55, 59
  Pombagira linked to, 8, 61, 63, 64, 74, 141
  Rangda compared to, 43
  studies of, 11, 143n10
  sweetening (dulcification) of, 6, 60–1, 62, 66
  and women's empowerment, 8, 59, 63, 64, 74
  yantras of, 63
  Yoruba religion compared to, 96
Kardec, Allan, 78, 88, 92, 150n23
Kinsley, David R., 55, 56
Kirill of Turov, Saint, 21
korowody (Slavic round dances), 19
Koshchey Bessmertnyi (Bony the Deathless), 18, 29, 34, 137

Kripal, Jeffrey J., 143n10
Kubitschek, Juscelino, 150–1n27

La Llorona, 120, 155n22
Lakṣmī (Hindu goddess), 1
Landes, Ruth, 101
Latin America, 5, 9
Leyes de Reforma (1859–1863), 129
Lilith, 140
liminality
  of Baba Yaga, 7, 9, 15–17, 19, 36, 39, 69, 133, 137, 138
  concept of, 3–4, 40
  divine feminine embodying, 1, 3, 5
  of Hermes, 72
  of Kālī, 69, 133, 137, 138
  of Pombagira, 69, 74, 75, 76, 85, 91–2, 98–101, 133, 137, 140
  of Santa Muerte, 8, 9, 69, 103, 113, 118, 123, 137, 138, 140
  spatial liminality, 9
  studies of, 10
  temporal liminality, 9
  Turner on, 3, 4, 5, 36, 143n1, 143n3
  of Umbanda religion, 91–2
  and Yoruba religion, 94, 96
Lithuania, 27, 28, 35, 145n20
Loki (Skandinavia), 72
Lopez, Alma, 154–5n21
López, Angélica, 119
López, Yolanda M., 154–5n21
López de Ayala, Pedro, 155n29
Lotería (lottery) cards, 156–7n36
Lula da Silva, Luiz Inácio, 151n27

Ma Mansa Devī, 27
macumbas, 87–8
magical powers and practices
  of Baba Yaga, 1, 5, 7, 17, 19, 21, 24, 30, 32, 33, 34, 35, 36, 37, 38, 45, 57, 139
  of Exu, 92
  of Kālī, 1, 5, 54, 56, 57, 139

  of Pombagira, 1, 5, 10, 74–5, 76, 77, 88, 98, 99, 132, 133, 134, 138, 139
  of Santa Muerte, 1, 5, 10, 110, 132, 133, 134, 138, 139
  of witches, 140
Mahānirvāna Tantra, 42
Mahāvidyās (Ten Great Wisdoms or Hindu goddesses), 54–6
Malleus Maleficarum (The Hammer of Witches), 140
Margaret, Saint, 145n23
marginality
  and Baba Yaga, 1, 3, 5, 9, 39, 138, 141, 142
  divine feminine embodying, 3, 5
  and Kālī, 1, 3, 5, 9, 54, 55, 56–7, 66, 138, 140–1, 142
  and liminality, 4
  and Pombagira, 1, 3, 5, 9, 69, 72, 74, 85, 92, 99, 100, 132, 134, 138, 139, 141, 142
  and Santa Muerte, 1, 3, 5, 8, 9, 69, 103, 116, 118, 120, 121–2, 123, 132, 134, 138, 139, 141, 142
  and Umbanda religion, 88–9, 91
Margolles, Teresa, 120
Maria Padilha (Pombagira), 76–7, 78, 81, 83, 92, 133
Marias Molambo (Raggedy Pombagiras), 75–6
Marie Jacobé, Saint, 149n6
Marie Salomé, Saint, 149n6
Márquez, Lenin, 120
Martenitsas, 31–2, 32
Martinez, Elda Evangelina Gonzalez, 88
Mary Magdalene, 149n6
Master of Erfurt, 51
matriarchy
  concept of, 147n38
  remnants of matriarchal rule, 43–4
matrilineal social structure, 44, 147n40
matrilocal societies, 44, 147n39

Mayan culture, 156n33
McDermott, Rachel Fell, 143n10
Mérimée, Prosper, 77
Mesa Branca ceremonies, 152n41
Mexican *colonias*, 4, 8, 103, 114
Mexico
  death in arts and folklore, 129–32
  Memento Mori tradition, 120
  Mexican society and death, 118–23
  Mexico City's Tepito neighborhood, 8, 103, 114, 117–18, 121
  Native Mexican societies, 9, 34, 103, 118, 127–8, 132
  outsiders of, 6–7
  see also Santa Muerte
Mexico-US borderlands, 4, 103, 113
Mictlantecuhtli and Mictecacíhuatl (Aztec Lord and Lady of Death), 127
migrations, 10
Minoan Snake Goddess, 27
Mokosh (Finno-Slavic goddess), 22–3, 41, 50, 51
Mother Goddess, 26, 37
Mother Moist Earth, 34, 46, 51
mountaintops, "baba" in names of, 23
mummification, 124
mushrooms, 38

NAFTA, 119
Nanã (iabá), 34, 73, 84, 97
National Day of the Gypsy People, Brazil, 151n27
Native American traditions, 38, 72, 89, 132
Ndembu culture of Zambia, 3, 15
neighborhoods
  Hispanic neighborhood *bodegas*, 112
  marginal neighborhoods, 8
  Nova Iguaçú neighborhood, Rio de Janeiro, 78
  peripheral neighborhoods, 5
  Quintino neighborhood, Rio de Janeiro, 80
  of Salvador da Bahia, Brazil, 70, 71
  Santo Antônio neighborhood, Salvador da Bahia, 71
  Tepito neighborhood, Mexico City, 8, 103, 114, 117–18, 121
  West Side neighborhood, San Antonio, 115
Neolithic era, 35, 36
New Age practices, 78, 79, 83
New Spain, 125–6, 129, 132
Nigeria, 70, 71, 93, 148–9n5
Nova Iguaçú neighborhood, Rio de Janeiro, Brazil, 78
number "three," as number of synthesis, 19–20

Obá (iabá), 73
Obatalá, 73, 149n8
Occultism, 88
Old European bird goddess, 24–5
Oleszkiewicz, Eligiusz, 145n20
Omolocô religion, 80, *93*
orixás (gods and goddesses)
  of Candomblé religion, 70, 74, 84, 86, 100, 101, 147n5, 148n3, 149n8
  Oxalá as, 79, 97, 149n8
  spiritual energy embodied by, 64
  sweetening (dulcification) of, 141
  of Umbanda religion, 90, 91, 107
  see also Àwọn Ìyá Wa (African ancestral mothers); Ìyàmi Òṣòròngà
Our Lady Aparecida, Brazil, 65, 78, *78*, 80, 134
Our Lady of Ostra Brama, Vilnius, Lithuania, 145n19
outsiderhood
  concept of, 4
  divine feminine embodying, 1, 2, 6
  and Kālī, 65
  and Pombagira, 72, 89
  and Santa Muerte, 103

owls, 25, 97, 104, 113
Oxalá, 79, 97, 149n8
Oxum (iabá), 1, 34, 73, 84

Padilla, María, 76–7
Paleolithic era, 19, 21, 25, 32, 36
pan-African belief systems
  and Àwọn Ìyá Wa, 39, 73, 74–5, 76, 84, 93, 94, 98
  and Ìyàmi Òṣoròngà, 8, 17, 20, 25, 30–1, 58, 59, 62, 75, 87, 97, 98–9, 146n24
  see also African/African-derived religions
paradox
  and Baba Yaga, 5, 16, 19, 61, 137
  and Kālī, 5, 55, 59, 61, 137
  and Pombagira, 5, 61, 137
  and Santa Muerte, 5, 61, 123, 137
Paraguay, 127, 152n51
Paraskeva Piatnitsa, Saint, 23, 41, 50–1
Parroquia de la Misericordia, 114–15
patriarchy, 34, 98–9
Pedro I of Castile, 76–7
pelicans, "baba" as name for, 23–4
Pentecostalism, 88
periphery
  and Baba Yaga, 56, 138, 141
  and Kālī, 56, 138, 141
  peripheral neighborhoods, 5
  and Pombagira, 56, 69, 78, 99, 138
  and Santa Muerte, 56, 69, 138, 141
Peru, mummies in, 144n7
Pio V (pope), 114
pisanki (painted eggs), 19
Poland
  dolls in, 144n7
  embroidery portraying goddess, 46, *47*
  feast names in, 23
  Marzanna in, 44–5, *45*
  paper cutouts portraying goddess, 46, *47*, *48*, *50*
  place-names in, 23

Polish language, 22, 23
Pombagira
  advice giving aspect of, 8, 63–4, 75, 147n5
  agency of, 101
  and ambiguity, 74–5, 85, 100, 134, 137, 141
  and Baba Yaga, 8, 15, 74
  characteristics of, 8, 72, 73–5
  devotional centers of, 78–81, 152n51
  devotions to, 63, 70, 132, 140
  duality of, 61, 75, 98, 99, 100
  dwelling places of, 8, 9, 75, 76, 85, 134, 137
  and Exu, 8, 33, 72, 85, 86
  as female trickster figure, 72, 86, 100
  as fierce feminine divinity, 1
  house altar, Salvador, Bahia, Brazil, *71*
  and judiciary case, 81
  Kālī linked to, 8, 61, 63, 64, 74, 141
  as lady of cemeteries, 9
  liminality of, 69, 74, 75, 76, 85, 91–2, 98–101, 133, 137, 138
  and marginality, 1, 3, 5, 9, 69, 72, 74, 85, 92, 99, 100, 132, 134, 138, 139, 141, 142
  as mediator, 88, 137
  as New World syncretic creation, 5
  offerings to, 134
  origins of, 72–3, 93–101, 132, 138
  pontos cantados (sacred songs) of, 63, 73–4, 77, 83, 89, 92, 132, 133, 149n9
  pontos riscados (sacred drawings), 63, 149n9
  as protector of women, 71, 73
  as sacred prostitute, 70, 74, 75, 148n2
  Santa Muerte compared to, 8, 10, 74, 76, 79, 99, 138–9
  as street spirit, 91, *91*, 92

Pombagira—*Continued*
and structural inferiority, 69, 74, 85, 88, 139
studies of, 10
symbols of, *82*
trances associated with, 8, 9–10, 63, 75, 147n5
types of, 75–7, 137
as witch, 8, 93
and women's empowerment, 8, 63, 64, 71, 93, 147n5
worshippers of, 7, 85–6, 88, 134, 138, 139
Pombagiras Ciganas (Gypsy Pombagiras), 75, 78, 83, 91
Pombagiras cruzadas da Linha das Almas (crossed Pombagiras of the Line of the Souls), 76
Pombagiras Meninas (Virgin Child Pombagiras), 76
Posada, José Guadalupe, 129–30
Potebnja, Aleksandr, 35
povo da rua (street spirits), 72, 91–2, *91*
pragmatism, 138, 139
Prandi, Reginaldo, 152n39
Prêtos Velhos, 80
Propp, Vladimir
on Baba Yaga's blindness, 22
on Baba Yaga's donor role, 17
on Baba Yaga's hut, 37, 144n4, 146n31
on dragons, 29, 30
on horses, 33
on initiation rituals, 21
on matriarchy, 43
on roles in Russian magical tales, 144n2
studies of Baba Yaga, 144n1
prostitutes and holy harlots, 8, 70, 74, 75, 89, 100, 148n2
Pulcinella (Italy), 72

Quetzalcoatl (feathered serpent), 28, *29*

Quimbanda religion, 80, 87, 91–2, 149n7
Quintino neighborhood, Rio de Janeiro, Brazil, 80

Ramirez, Anrez. *See* Vidal, João Marcelo
Rāmprasād (Bengali poet-saint), 61, 62
Rangda (Balinese witch), 43
Regla de Ocha (Santería)
and cigar smoke, 89
goddess as trinity in, 34
and Santa Muerte, 79, 106–7, 111, 116
and Yemayá, 135, 152n49
Reynard the fox, 72
rites of passage
Baba Yaga's role in, 7, 21, 22, 37, 38–9, 40, 137
and liminality, 3
and Santa Muerte, 103
Rivera, Diego, 129–30
Roma, 64, 66, 77, 83, 108, 132, 149n6, 150–1n27, 153n6
Romani diaspora, 66
Romero, Enriqueta, 107, 112, 114, 115
Romo Guillén, David, 106, 112, 114, 115, 153n4
Rorarni, Miriam Stanescon, 151n27
Rulfo, Juan, 156–7n36
Rusałki, 34, 35, 46, 51
Russian language, 6, 22, 26, 33, 41, 42, 44, 46
Russian *volshebnye skazki* (magical tales), 7, 17–21, 25

sacred prostitution, 148n2
see also holy harlots and prostitutes
sacrifice
animal sacrifice, 61, 73, 89, 151n39
blood sacrifice, 8, 9, 63, 64, 74, 75, 139
human sacrifice, 35, 56–7, 113, 127
Salinas de Gortari, Carlos, 119

San Antonio, Texas
  Altar for the Dead, *129*, 130
  botánicas of, *109*, 111, 115–16,
    116, 154n13
  Lowrider, Lowrider Festival, 130
  Lowrider trunk altar for the dead,
    131, *131*
  and Santa Muerte, 155n26
San Cristóbal de Las Casas, Mexico,
  botánica of, 115, *117*
San Luis de Paz, Guanajuato, 126
San Pascualito Rey or San Pascual
  Bailón, Tuxtla Gutiérrez,
  Chiapas, 126, 156n31
Santa Muerte
  advice giving aspect of, 64
  and ambiguity, 120, 134, 137, 141
  artistic representations of, 105, 108
  and Baba Yaga, 15
  characteristics of, 112
  devotional centers of, 114–18,
    155n26
  devotions to, 10, 103, 104, 105,
    106, 107–8, 111–14, 115, 116,
    117–18, 119, 120, 121–3,
    132, 133, 139, 140, 155n24,
    155n25
  duality of, 61, 120
  dwelling place of, 9, 134
  and everyday survival, 121–2
  as fierce feminine divinity, 1
  historical antecedents of, 123–8
  iconography of, 2, 104, 105, 123,
    125, 126, 127
  Kālī compared to, 61, 63
  liminality of, 8, 9, 69, 103, 113,
    118, 123, 137, 138, 140
  and love magic, 10
  and marginality, 1, 3, 5, 8, 9, 69,
    103, 116, 118, 120, 121–2, 123,
    132, 134, 138, 139, 141, 142
  as mediator, 112–13, 137
  names of, 108, 153–4n7
  narcoaltares to, 113–14
  offerings to, 107, *109*, 134
  origins of, 103

Pombagira compared to, 8, 10,
    74, 76, 79, 99, 138–9
  portrayals of, 104–8, *104*, *105*,
    106, *107*, *108*, 110–11, *110*, *111*
  on products, 108, *109*
  as skeleton, 9
  statue materials, 108, 154n8
  studies of, 143n10
  and syncretism, 105, 112, 113,
    116, 121, 134
  twofold nature of, 98
  as Virgin of Guadalupe, 110, *111*
  worshippers of, 7, 134, 138, 139
Santería. *See* Regla de Ocha
  (Santería)
Santo Antônio neighborhood,
  Salvador da Bahia, Brazil, 71
Sara Kali, Santa
  on altar, Tzara Ramirez, Rio de
    Janeiro, Brazil, *78*
  as Brazilian version of Sara-La-Kâli,
    149n6
  and Catholic Church, 65, 78,
    149n6
  Pombagira compared to, 72, 75,
    78, 83–4, 99, 134
  and Roma people, 153n6
  Santa Muerte compared to, 108
  and Umbanda religion, 80
Sara-La-Kâli, Les Saintes
  Maries-de-la-Mer, France,
  64, *65*, 149n6
sexuality
  Baba Yaga connected to, 1, 5, 16,
    43, 51, 137, 140
  Kālī connected to, 1, 5, 6, 56, 63,
    74, 137–8, 140
  Pombagira connected to, 1, 5, 10,
    63, 72, 73, 74, 75, 76, 98, 99,
    134, 137, 138, 140
  Santa Muerte connected to, 1, 5,
    118, 121, 134, 137, 138, 140
Siberian male shamans, 42
Singer, Isaac Bashevis
  The King of the Fields, 34–5
  Stories for Children, 35

Slavic languages, 26, 44
Slavic traditions
  Baba Yaga's name unique to, 22, 145n13
  and bear as mediator, 33
  and bird symbols, 25, 97
  and burial rituals, 38
  Christmas Carol, 49–50, 97
  embroidery, 46, *47*, *48*, 49–50, *49*
  folktales, 18, 19, 20, 22, 30, 33, 35, 36, 38, 39, 40, 43–4, 44, 137, 144n7
  goddess as trinity in, 34, 46
  and Martenitsas, 31–2, *32*
  and Mother Earth, 19
  and *pisanki* (painted eggs), 19
  and snake symbols, 28
  and witches, 41–2
Slovakia, 23
Slovenia, 23
snake goddesses, 25, 27, 28
snakes and serpents
  and Baba Yaga, 17, 20, 26, 27, 28, 35
  and Bhadrakālī, 62
  birds associated with, 27
  and Coatlicue, 61, 143n2
  dragons associated with, 28, 29
  as guardians of Waters of Life, 28
  Kālī associated with, 61
  as mediators, 20, 27–8
  Quetzalcoatl as feathered serpent, 28, *29*
  as self-renovating beings, 35
  as symbols of Mother Earth, 26
  and transformation, 27
  and Virgin Mary, 30
Sokovic, Maya
  Baba Yaga, *16*
  Kālī, *60*
South-Central Asia, 5
Spinosaurus, 145n22
Spiritism, 78, 88, 92, 93, *93*, 150n23
Stomma, L., 51
Stone Babas (Scynthian and Finno-Ugric origin), 45–6
street spirits (*povo da rua*), 72, 91–2, *91*
structural inferiority
  concept of, 4
  divine feminine embodying, 1
  and Pombagira, 69, 74, 85, 88, 139
  and Santa Muerte, 139
  and Umbanda religion, 92
subaltern classes, 7, 74, 139, 140
sweetening (dulcification)
  of divine feminine, 5, 6, 60–1, 62, 66, 84, 99, 100, 134–5, 141
  of Iemanjá, 84, *84*, 99, 100, 134–5, 141
  of Kālī, 6, 60–1, 62, 66
syncretism and syncretic religions
  in Brazil, 70–1, 78–9
  and Catholic Church, 65
  and goddess as trinity, 34
  and Santa Muerte, 105, 112, 113, 116, 124, 134
  studies of, 10
  syncretism of Virgin Mary and Iemanjá, 84
  Umbanda religion as, 70–1, 79–80, 88, 93, 149n7, 150n23
Szafrański, Włodzimierz, 18, 21, 38
Szakolczai, Arpad, 3
Szyjewski, Andrzej, 23, 28

Tanit (Carthaginian goddess), 25
Tantrism, 54, 55–6
Tapís de la creació (Tapestry of Creation), Girona Cathedral, Spain, 23, *24*
Tārā (Hindu goddess), 54, 55
Taussig, Michael, 100
Templo dos Ciganos Encantados, 80
Tepito neighborhood, Mexico City, 8, 103, 114, 117–18, 121
Thomassen, Bjorn, 3
thresholds
  and Baba Yaga, 9, 29, 36, 40, 57, 69, 137
  and Kālī, 57, 69

and liminality, 3, 5, 40
and Pombagira, 75, 99
The Thunder, Perfect Mind (Gnostic text), 58, 59, 95–6, 99
Tlazolteotl (Aztec goddess), 75
Toci (Aztec deity), 34
tombs
and Baba Yaga's hut as tomb, 16, 19, 35–41
of deceased noble individuals, 124
Tonantzin (Aztec deity), 34
Toporov, V. N., 17, 18, 37, 144n1
Torres, João de, 150n27
trances
Kālī associated with, 8, 9–10, 63–4, 74
Pombagira associated with, 8, 9–10, 63, 75, 81, 89, 147n5
transculturation, 10
transformation
Baba Yaga associated with, 7, 10, 19, 36, 39, 57, 58, 69
divine feminine's power over, 1
horses associated with, 34
Kālī associated with, 55, 57, 62, 69
Santa Muerte associated with, 116
snakes associated with, 27
witch archetype associated with, 6
transnationality, of Santa Muerte, 9, 115
tree of life, 46, *49*
Trinidad, Kālī devotion in, 64, 66, 141
trinities, 19–20
trinity of goddesses, 19, 34, 46
Turner, Victor
on colors, 31, 83
on liminality, 3, 4, 5, 36, 143n1, 143n3
on Ndembu culture of Zambia, 3, 15
Tzara Ramirez religious center, Rio de Janeiro, Brazil, 78–9, *78, 79, 80, 81, 82*

Ukraine, house snakes in, 27
Umbanda religion
continuum of, 92–3, *93*, 99
entidades of, 90–1
and everyday survival, 85
and Exu, 79, 85–6, 87, 88, 91, 97
liminality of, 91–2
Mesa Branca ceremonies, 152n41
offerings of, 89, *90*
orixás of, 90, 91, 107
and religious communities, 87, 89
and ritual animal sacrifice, 89, 152n39
and Santa Muerte, 107
and Sara Kali, 80
spread of, 152n51
and structural inferiority, 92
as syncretic religion, 70–1, 79–80, 88, 93, 134, 149n7, 150n23
and trances, 89, 151n38
see also Pombagira
Uruguay, 72, 152n51
Uspienskij, Boris, 22–3

van Gennep, Arnold, 3
Vedic religion, 33
veladoras (votive candles), 107, *109*
Velázquez, Diego, 26
Verger, Pierre, 97
viburnum opulus, 28
Vidal, João Marcelo, 79, *80, 81, 82*
Virgin Mary
Annunciation of Our Lady, 33
Assumption of the Virgin Mary, 114
as benign female divinity, 1, 63
doves associated with, 26, 97
Eve as opposite of, 150n18
grottos as sanctuaries of, 36, 51
guardianship of cities, 145n19
Kālī identified with, 64, 66
as Mother Moist Earth, 51
Our Lady Aparecida, 65, 78, *78*, 80, 134
Our Lady of Ostra Brama, 145n19
Pombagira compared to, 99

Virgin Mary—*Continued*
  as protective mother, 157n1
  Saint Paraskeva Piatnitsa in
    opposition to, 50–1
  and Santa Muerte, 105
  and snakes, 30
  syncretism with Iemanjá, 84
  Virgen de las Mercedes, 149n8
  Virgin of Guadalupe, 110, *111*,
    112, 115, 119, 120, 134, 139,
    154–5n21
Vladimir of Kiev, Prince, 51
vultures, 25

War on Drugs, 119
Washington, Teresa N., 41, 83, 95
Week of Gypsy Culture, Brazil,
  151n27
West Indies, Kālī worshipped in, 5, 7
West Side neighborhood, San
  Antonio, Texas, 115
Western culture, values of, 6, 101
White Goddess, 40
wildness
  Kālī associated with, 54, 55, 64,
    69, 138, 141
  Pombagira associated with, 138,
    141
witches
  Baba Yaga as witch, 35, 41–5,
    51–2
  bird companions of, 97
  bruxas, 93, 98, 132, 152n42
  etymology of witch, 6, 41, 42
  fierce feminine divinity connected
    to, 6
  and Pombagira, 8, 93
  women identified as, 140, 151n32
womb
  Baba Yaga associated with, 23,
    69, 133
  and Baba Yaga's hut, 16, 19,
    35–41
  Kālī associated with, 63, 69, 133
  and liminality, 5

Pombagira associated with, 63,
  77, 133
women
  demonization of, 140
  exclusion from religious posts, 43
  identified as witches, 140, 151n32
  as shamans, 140
  Western model for, 1–2
women's empowerment
  and Kālī, 8, 59, 63, 64, 74
  and Pombagira, 8, 63, 64, 71, 93,
    147n5
worshippers
  of Kālī, 65–6, 139
  marginality of, 3, 5, 7, 8–9, 66,
    69, 91
  of Pombagira, 7, 85–6, 88, 134,
    138, 139
  of Santa Muerte, 7, 134, 138, 139

Xochiquetzal (Aztec goddess), 34

Yanhuitlán, Oaxaca, 126
Yankov, Yanko A., 146n28
yaxche tree, 145n21
Yemayá. *See* Iemanjá/Yemayá
  (queen of the oceans)
Yemoja, 135
Yoruba people, as slaves in Brazil,
  148–9n5
Yoruba religion
  ancestral Mothers of, 41, 43,
    93–7, 98, 152n47
  myths of, 100
  practice of, 100
  and Santa Muerte, 111
  and syncretism, 34
  Yemoja, 135
  see also pan-African belief systems

Zé Pilintra (Exu), 72, *81*, 87, 91,
  151n34
Zedillo, Ernesto, 119
Złota Baba (Golden Woman), 50
Żywa (Polish goddess), 50, *50*

The manufacturer's authorised representative in the EU is Springer Nature Customer Service Centre GmbH, Europaplatz 3, 69115 Heidelberg, Germany. If you have any concerns regarding our products, please contact ProductSafety@springernature.com

Printed and bound by CPI Group (UK) Ltd, Croydon, CR0 4YY

23/03/2026

02076398-0005